Jade Mirror
Women Poets of China

Jade Mirror

Women Poets of China

Translated by
Grace Fong, Emily Goedde,
Jeanne Larsen, Geoffrey Waters
and Michael Farman

WHITE PINE PRESS / BUFFALO, NEW YORK

White Pine Press
P.O. Box 236, Buffalo, New York 14201
www.whitepine.org

Acknowledgments: Michael Farman would like to express his gratitude to the
editors of the following journals in which some of these translations first
appeared: Shijing: *Renditions* Number 66; Zi Ye: *eXchanges 2007, Circumference;* Li
Qingzhao: *Two Lines XIV*

Jeanne Larsen's Xue Tao translations first appeared in *Brocade River Poems,*
Princeton University Press, 1987. She expresses her thanks to the editors for per-
mission to reprint some of them.

Grace Fong wishes to thank the editors of the following journals in which
these poems appeared in earlier versions: Two Poems by Ji Xian: *Early Modern
Women: an Interdisciplinary Journal* (2007); Lu Bicheng: *Nan Nu: Men, Women and Gender
in China* 6.1 (2004). She also thanks the editors of University of Hawaii Press for
permission to reprint poems by Shen Cai from her book *Herself an Author: Gender,
Agency, and Writing in Late Imperial China* (2008)

Publication of this book was made possible, in part, by grants from
Amazon.com and the National Endowment for the Arts, which believes that a
great nation deserves great art; and with public funds from the New York State
Council on the Arts, a State Agency.

Cover art: Li Zi Hou

First Edition.

ISBN: 978-1-935210-49-8

Printed and bound in the United States of America.

Library of Congress Control Number: 2013947485

CONTENTS

INTRODUCTION

MICHAEL FARMAN

Poetry has always occupied a status ... that accorded to it in Western countr... country's long history it was regarded ... province. From the Han Dynasty (206 ... ...ually the only route for men to secure emp... ...as through the Imperial Examinations, in which candidates were required to demonstrate an encyclopedic knowledge of treasured literature and to show skill and artistry by adding to the literary heritage. Composing verse was therefore not only the preferred means by which men chose to express themselves and communicate with each other, it was also a vital accomplishment for avoiding a life of poverty. Since women, with a few exceptions, were excluded from public office and forbidden by law to take the examinations, their literary talents often remained hidden. A pointer to prevailing attitudes, at least until post-medieval times, can be found in one of the most famous collections from the period commonly regarded as the greatest flowering of Chinese culture: the *Three Hundred Tang Poems,* in which just one poem by a woman is included.

Young women were brought up in isolation from male society. Those who became wives were expected to stay at home, do household chores and bear children; their education did not normally extend beyond acquiring the skills for these duties. In such a society, who were the women who managed to find a poetic voice? Fortunately, there were always a few who beat the odds and made immeasurable contributions to China's poetic heritage. They came from diverse areas of society: some were from families that were prestigious and wealthy enough to ensure a literary education for their women; Li Qingzhao is the most famous example. There were courtesans who moved freely in the upper levels of society, often on familiar terms with male scholar-poets. Xue Tao, represented here, is one such. Many male literati would be attracted to courtesans who could converse and correspond with them on equal terms; the poetry of Xue Tao and Yu Xuanji often celebrates such interactions.

Other voices are also heard: palace concubines, struggling to create significance in what was essentially a life of enforced confinement and idleness, were sometimes drawn to create poetry. The concubines kept by scholar-officials probably had more creative leisure time than wives to develop literary talent. At another social level were women of the entertainment districts of the great cities, skilled in music, dancing, conversation; their company was sought by the male literati and their exotic music sometimes inspired men to compose new lyrics to the music, often invoking the persona of a woman. Women poets were later to use this genre for their own expressive purposes. Arguably the most liberated women of all were Buddhist and Daoist nuns who were freer to form a spectrum of relationships with both sexes and compose verses celebrating friendships and loves.

These social categories were not mutually exclusive; distinctions could be blurred and occupations overlap. Yu Xuanji, for example, one of our chosen poets, began her young adult life as an entertainment girl, but became the concubine of a scholar, and later still a Daoist nun.

There is a further category in which two of our chosen poets must be placed: that of enigma. There is little or no information beyond the poems themselves to shed light on the 4th Century poet known as Zi Ye (Woman of the Night) or to authenticate the identity and life of the great Song Dynasty poet Zhu Shuzhen. Although these works are entirely convincing as expressions of feminine sensibility, such was the popularity of cultivating a female persona among male poets that some commentators have postulated that men were responsible. The reader must decide what to believe.

Another question needs to be addressed: Are we to assume that the emotions expressed in the poems are genuinely those of the poet, or simply the voice of an adopted persona? The suffering of a woman left alone, abandoned by her husband or lover, frequently away running the Empire in some distant province, or just out philandering, was a very popular subject. We should be cautious about regarding the result as "subjective" in the way we read much Western romantic poetry. This is not to claim that the emotions are never genuine, just that (especially with the *ci* song lyrics), we can never be sure whether the author is role-playing. Consequently there is a danger in assuming autobiographical detail from the poetry without corroboration from other sources—a pitfall that has not been avoided by some well-known translators and commentators.

•

Unlike many other anthologies, this collection features only twelve poets, some well-known, others whom we consider deserving of wider appreciation. They are chosen from periods ranging from the earliest known collection to the 20th Century, spanning well over two thousand years. Within the limits of the book size, restricting the number of poets enables us to include more poems from those who created a large body of work. This works well for poets such as Zhu Shuzhen, who is often characterized as a purveyor of deep misery on the strength of the same few *ci* poems included in anthologies. Here, I am delighted to say that Emily Goedde's translations of a selection of her many *shi* prove that she has a wider range of emotional expression.

It is not absolutely necessary to be aware of the traditional Chinese poetic forms to enjoy these translations, but to know a little about them will certainly enhance the appreciation of what our translators are doing. One virtue of this anthology is that it demonstrates the varied ways the works can be presented in vibrant contemporary English. So what follows are some notes on the forms of the originals, roughly in the order that they became adopted.

The earliest collection, the *Book of Odes* (*Shijing*), was compiled before China existed as a unified country. A large part of this collection consists of songs and verses from the regions that made up a loose association of royal and feudal states. Among these poems known as the Airs of the States and the Odes, women express their loves, sorrows, and occupations with an uninhibited frankness, contrasting strongly with the more formally sophisticated verses of later centuries. These ancient poems have all the characteristics of folk poetry: the number of words per line, the length of the poem and the rhyming scheme may all vary widely; choruses and repeated lines are prominent. After the time of Confucius, familiarity with the contents of the *Book of Odes* came to be an essential part of a gentleman's education and a guide to moral conduct. The collection is still influential and taught widely.

The poetry featured next in this collection, from the 4th Century CE and traditionally claimed to be by the enigmatic Zi Ye, is invariably in rhyming quatrains, with each line having five characters. Within the compass of those twenty characters the poet sings frankly of love in a way that contradicts pundits who have claimed that Chinese poetry lacks erotic expression. These poems were often imitated later, particularly by some well-known poets of the Tang Dynasty, and it is possible that some of those imitations have found their way into the collection as we know it today.

The *gushi*, or Ancient Verse, dates from around 300 CE, and is relatively free in form, usually with five or seven characters per line and no constraints on the number of lines to the poem. This length flexibility made it particularly suitable for narrative verse, and it was used thus by some of the great poets of the Tang Dynasty. Included in our anthology is a *gushi* by China's only Empress Regnant, Wu Zhao.

A new and influential genre evolved from about 500 CE, known as the *lushi* or Regulated Verse. It followed far stricter rules than the earlier forms and was required to have eight lines arranged as four couplets of either five or seven characters in length, in which the spoken tones followed a strict pattern and the rhyming scheme was predetermined. Another defining feature was the parallelism of words between paired lines in the central couplets. A sub-genre of the *lushi* was the *jueju*, or quatrain, in which the poem's length was reduced to four lines following the same tonal and rhyming rules as the *lushi* but without the parallelisms. Such poetry was considered the highest form of aesthetic expression, and from the early Tang Dynasty on, mastery of these two verse forms was the mark of an educated gentleman. The collection known as the *300 Tang Poems* contains many of the most famous examples of this genre. Their expressive range includes "harmonizing" with the poems of friends or earlier poets by following the same rhymes and tonal patterns, writing letters in verse form, recording a meeting or a farewell, and sometimes the dangerous practice of criticizing the current administration by disguising the barbs as references to famous past events or as nature imagery. Women poets taking up this form used it in broadly similar ways, but often with greater emphasis on subjectivity; nature imagery could also be simply just that, the expression of enjoyment of the beauty of the world.

The final genre represented here differs from the others in that it consists of words composed to fit existing song patterns. It is the *ci*, or song lyric, that became popular in the entertainment quarters of the capital and other major cities in the early days of the Tang Dynasty. Male scholar poets who were the clients of the singing girls would sometimes compose their own lyrics to fit the melodies; the practice caught on, reaching its heyday in the Northern and Southern Song Dynasties. The men would often adopt a female voice to personify their favorite erotic image of the suffering woman. When women took up this poetic form they naturally found it appropriate for their own expressive purpose, although the fundamental nature of the *ci* remained that of a conceit, to be admired and moved by, but not necessarily that of an introspective confessional.

•

Although it is often said that much is lost in translating a pictographic and tonal language such as Chinese into a Western language, there is also something to be gained in the flexibility of approach this gives translators. One of the great pleasures in putting this collection together was enjoying the contrasting ways in which our translators have met the challenge of recreating the poetry in vibrant contemporary English.

In the following pages you will encounter the verses of women poets exemplifying all the categories listed above. The earliest anonymous voices, a mysterious "woman of the night," two women who exceptionally but briefly rose to the most powerful positions in the nation, a great poet of sorrow about whose life almost nothing is known, the woman poet acknowledged to be China's greatest, courtesans, concubines, Buddhist and Daoist priestesses, a talented woman of letters from a recently rediscovered golden period for educated women, and a powerful voice from the early 20th Century.

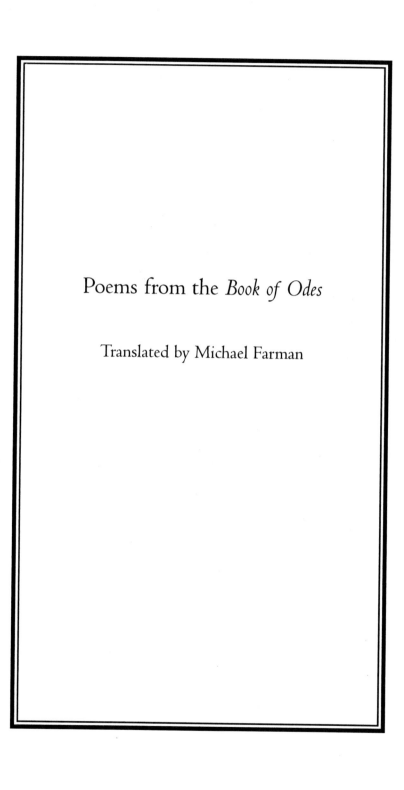

Poems from the *Book of Odes*

Translated by Michael Farman

Note on the Selection from the *Book of Odes*.

China's oldest surviving and most revered collection of poetry, the *Shijing*, or *Book of Odes*, dates from about 600 BCE, while some of the songs included are thought to have been already hundreds of years old at the time of collection. At these times a loose and widespread federation of feudal states was ruled by a series of kings from a capital near the present-day Xi'an (later moving to Luoyang). Each state was presided over by a hereditary lord with at least a nominal allegiance to the king. One theory for the collection's origin holds that the reigning king sent a squad of scholars out to record the poetry of the people in order to gauge their political allegiance. Another almost certainly incorrect belief is that Confucius was responsible for compiling the anthology. What is undeniable is that when it eventually became one of the Five Confucian Classics, it was regarded as a paradigm for correct conduct and morality. It became a powerful influence on later literature and remains widely read and taught in schools to this day.

If the verses were recorded on bamboo strips, they might well have been consigned to the flames by the notorious Shi Huang Di, the First Emperor of Qin. Fortunately, because the collection had been held to exemplify Confucian ethical principles, it had become required learning for all would-be officials; it could therefore be reconstructed from collective memory. In this process, there's no knowing how much conscious and unconscious editing took place, and some poems are clearly fragments. By the time of the Han Dynasty, (206 BCE to 220 CE) the revival of Confucian thought led to the publishing of three separate versions of the *Shijing*, complete with commentaries and interpretations. Ironically, the only version to have survived is a fourth unofficial text compiled by one Mao Heng. Today's versions are all based on this text; they generally adopt Master Mao's classification and numbering system.

The complete anthology is divided into four sections, namely, the "Airs of the States" (*Guofeng*), the "Minor Odes" (*Xiao ya*), the

17

"Greater Odes" (*Da ya*) and the "Hymns" (*Mao shi*), totaling 305 songs. The songs in the present selection are from the various regions represented in the first section. The "Airs" are by far the most interesting poems in the anthology, both as poetry and as a window into the society of the time. They are clearly from an oral tradition and reflect the lives of ordinary people; women's voices, singing of love, loss, sorrows, joys, work and play, are strongly represented. The nature of the poetry as folk-songs is borne out by the typical verse structure, in which lines are repeated in subsequent stanzas, often with just a few end-rhyming words changed, a structure characteristic of improvisation, repetition and erosion by time. Unlike the more sophisticated later poetry, there is no fixed number of characters per line or stanza length; the number of stanzas also varies. In many, each verse starts with a *xing*, a couplet containing some description from nature, which often (but not always) relates to what follows. This formulaic structure would have made it easy for even an uneducated (but not untalented) performer to extemporise a new song and for a listener to remember it.

The scarcity of pronouns in ancient Chinese often leads to ambiguity in identifying the gender of the speaker, and consequently to different interpretations of a poem. For this collection I have selected only those poems where the context gives high confidence that the voice is that of a woman.

MEF

Plantain Gathering Song

Picking plucking plantains!
        Now we're lifting them.
Plucking picking plantains!
        Now we have a few.

Plantain picking plucking!
        Now we're sorting them.
Plantain plucking picking!
        Now we smooth them out.

Plucking picking plantains!
        Now we hold them up.
Picking plucking plantains!
        Now we tuck them in our aprons.

Cicadas

How cicadas chattered,
how katydids were jumping!
I couldn't find my man
and how my heart is aching!
If only I could see him,
if only I could be with him
my heart would be at rest.

Climbing that southern hill,
I went to gather bracken.
I couldn't find my man
and how my heart is grieving!
If only I could see him,
if only I could be with him
my heart would now be singing.

Climbing that southern hill,
I went to gather ferns.
I couldn't find my man
and how my heart is shattered!
If only I could see him,
if only I could be with him
my heart would be at peace.

Plucking Plums

Plucking plums!
Just seven left.
Of all the gentlemen who court me,
one may have a lucky day!

Plucking plums!
Three more to go.
Of all the gentlemen who court me
one had better come today!

Plucking plums!
They're in the basket.
Of all the gentlemen who court me
one had better speak out now!

Cypress Wood Boat

A young woman is betrothed against her will.

A drifting cypress boat
is helpless, captive to the tide.
In my distress, I find no sleep,
haunted by this secret grief.
It's not because I have no wine,
nor idle time to come and go.

My heart is not a mirror
to reflect the will of others.
My brothers, young and old
how can I call on them?
I dare not speak my mind
for fear I'd make them angry.

My heart is not a stone
to be turned over;
my heart is not a mat
to be rolled away.
I bear myself with dignity;
what other choice have I?

Disguising my distress
from the scorn of lesser people,
I've still encountered trouble,
endured my share of insults.
I hold my tongue in silence,
but waking, beat my fist.

Great sun and moon
why do you come and go,
while misery still clings to me
like unwashed clothes?
Suffering in solitude,
I can't rise up and fly away.

Gathering the Beggarweed

Gathering the beggarweed
among the meadows of the Mei,
what man is on my mind?
That handsome eldest son of Jiang!
    Make a date in Sanzhong,
    meet me in Shanguan
    and say goodbye on the banks of the Qi.

Gathering the barleycorn
along the north side of the Mei,
what man is on my mind?
That handsome eldest son of Yi!
    Make a date in Sanzhong,
    meet me in Shanguan
    and say goodbye on the banks of the Qi.

Gathering the turnip-rape
along the east side of the Mei,
what man is on my mind?
That handsome eldest son of Yong!
    Make a date in Sanzhong,
    meet me in Shanguan
    and say goodbye on the banks of the Qi.

My Lord

My lord is full of swagger!
His left hand holds a reed-pipe,
his right hand gestures to my room.
Sheer delight!

My lord is so high-spirited!
His left hand holds a feather streamer,
his right hand bids me follow.
Sheer delight!

Please Mr. Zhong

Please Mr. Zhong
don't come bursting through my village,
don't break my willow tree!
It doesn't trouble me,
but I'm scared of what my folks will say.
I care about you, Mr. Zhong,
but parent's words
are truly to be dreaded.

Please Mr. Zhong
don't come crashing over the wall,
don't break my mulberry tree!
It doesn't trouble me,
but I'm scared of what my brothers say.
I care about you, Mr. Zhong,
but brothers' words
are truly to be dreaded.

Please Mr. Zhong
don't come smashing through my courtyard,
don't break my sandalwood tree!
It doesn't trouble me
but I'm scared that people gossip.
I care about you, Mr. Zhong,
but village gossip
is truly to be dreaded.

Crazy Boy!

That crazy boy won't speak to me!
Because of him, I'm off my food.

That crazy boy won't dine with me!
Because of him, I lie awake.

If You Should Care

If you should care for me young man
I'll lift my skirt and wade across the Qin;
but if your heart is somewhere else,
other men are out there,
            stupid boy!

If you should care for me young man
I'll raise my skirt and wade across the Wei;
but if your heart is somewhere else,
other men are waiting,
            stupid boy!

Bundling the Kindling

Bundling the kindling!
Orion's stars hang in the sky.
Tonight, tonight could be the night,
the night I meet my future man.
Oh my! oh my!
What will my future man be like?

Bundling the kindling!
Orion's stars are close at hand.
Tonight, tonight could be the night,
the night I face my destiny.
Oh my! oh my!
What will my destiny be like?

Bundling the kindling!
Orion's stars are at the door.
Tonight, tonight could be the night,
the night I find my shining star.
Oh my! oh my!
What will my shining star be like?

The Cloth-Vine

The cloth-vine grows on thorn-trees,
the tea-vine thrives in thickets.
Now my lovely one is gone,
who lives with me?
I live alone.

The cloth-vine flourishes on brambles,
the tea-vine spreads in meadows.
Now my lovely one is gone,
who lies with me?
I lie alone.

This splendid horn-shaped pillow,
this fine embroidered quilt!
Now my lovely one is gone,
who wakes with me?
I wake alone.

Days of winter,
nights of summer.
A lifetime waiting
to be with him again.

Nights of winter,
days of summer.
A lifetime waiting
to lie with him again.

The Falcon

The falcon breasts the morning breeze
above those gloomy northern trees.
I haven't met my future master,
my heart is dreading some disaster!
How can it be, how can it be
that he forgets to come to me?

On mountain slopes, the great oaks clump;
the motley trees prefer the swamp.
I haven't met my future lord,
my anxious heart awaits his word!
How can it be, how can it be
that he forgets to speak to me?

White poplar trees grow on the hill;
in marshland wild pears flourish still.
I haven't met my promised mate,
my heart reels in a drunken state!
How can it be, how can it be,
that he forgets to lie with me?

Lamb's Wool Coat

Carefree in your lamb's wool coat,
formal in your fox fur,
how could I not be smitten?
Oh, the agony!

Idle in your lamb's wool coat,
festive in your fox fur,
how could I not be smitten?
Oh, the torment!

Shining in your lamb's wool coat,
splendid as the sunrise,
how could I not be smitten?
Oh, the suffering!

White-Cap Boy

White-cap-boy,
how many times I've seen you
only to feel confused and tongue-tied,
sadder than before.

White-coat-boy,
how many times I've seen you
only to nurse my wounded heart,
longing to be with you.

Boy-in-white,
how many times I've seen you
only to find my heart in knots,
wishing us together.

Zi Ye Ge

Midnight Songs

Translated by Jeanne Larsen & Michael Farman

At some time in the fourth century, a collection of 117 quatrains appeared in a publication by the *Yue Fu*, or Music Bureau. This institution was founded by the great Emperor Wu of the Han Dynasty to promote music and poetry and continued to flourish for centuries later. The quatrains were described as the *Zi Ye Ge* or "Songs of the Person of the Night." The lyrics introduce us to the life and passions of a courtesan or a wine-shop girl, but there is no evidence for the poet's existence beyond that contained in the songs themselves. Scholars and commentators still debate the nature of the poetry's origins; some maintain that the consistency of the poetry is evidence for a single female author; others point to the strong later tradition of collective contributions by scholar-poets to lyrics with a female persona, to conclude that "Zi Ye" (c. 350 CE) may simply be a description of a collective genre. Whatever the truth, the strength of the personality that emerges from these lyrics lends imaginative reality and a powerful presence; I think it will be easy for readers to recognize the experiences and feelings portrayed in the poems as familiar and truthful.

The songs are all in the form of single quatrains with five characters per line. The almost invariable rhyming pattern is A-B-C-B. This concise form, and the presence of rhyme, combine to give them an epigrammatic quality. The emotional range encompasses sorrow, humor, joy in life, love of nature and above all a lyrical eroticism often conveyed by the sly use of euphemisms and double-entendres. Nature imagery carries much of the emotional charge; falling blossoms, spring winds, lotus seeds, are examples of images employed to convey meanings that resonate beyond the nature-descriptive. Although this imagery could be characterized as euphemistic, it is far less inhibited and more explicit than that of love poetry from later Dynasties.

The Zi Ye collection is, I believe, best perceived as a life-enhancing contribution to a tradition of Chinese love poetry as old as the civilization. The erotic vein in Chinese literature had often passed unnoticed, many early translators either failed to perceive or deliberately ignored it. However, these lyrics have resonated powerfully with many later poets who were moved to produce their own imitations of the Zi Ye quatrains; their influence continued and flourished, above all in the more sophisticated *ci* lyrics of the Tang and Song Dynasties.

M E F

Ever since we
parted, love,
I've not once opened
my make-up case.

> My head's a wreck.
> I don't comb it.
> Powder flurries:
> more dust on my clothes.

Ever since we
parted, lover,
when's the day
I haven't sighed?

Bitterwood trees
grow thick, a forest now.
How's it right—so
much, so much gone sour?

Plant his-face lotuses high
among the peaks? You'll
have to make your way
past Bitterwood Fort.

       Come time to pluck
       just one lovely
       bloom—go far
       and wide: you'll get
       nothing as sweet.

I take my pillow, lie down
by the back window.
You come, lover,
come close. We play.

    A little bliss.
    So much that's rough
    and rude. This love
    of ours, just how
    long can it last?

Love, when you're
unhappy, I
turn sad. Smile and
it's my joy.

Haven't you seen
two trees growing
close? From different
roots, they rise, limbs
inter-twined.

Who could feel like this
and not make songs?
Who can hunger
and not eat?

Day fades. I lean
against the doorjamb:
depressed, regretful, recalling
everything.

Where, love, did you
come from, looking
like a decent man
with a melancholy air?

Three times I call. Not
one response. Then how
are you like true cedars,
or the pine trees,
ever green?

The air is fresh.
The clear moon glows.
All night with you,
my lord: we have our fun.

    Sing out, lover,
    that subtle tune,
    and I'll let loose
    a musky
    flow of words.

I play the north
star's part—
a thousand years
and steady in my course.

     Love, your heart
     goes like the sun.
     Mornings, east. Come
     dusk, you've
     moved on west.

When I count on love,
it's like I'm ready
to move in close.
But, shy, I won't
risk forwardness.

A mouth made red:
arousing songs
pour out. White jade
fingers stroke
those sensitive strings.

Translations by Michael Farman:

sleepless through
the long night
troubled by
the moon's glare

I thought I heard
a distant voice
and promised yes
to empty air

moonlight gleams
through cassia woods
where radiant flowers
bud and bloom

at times like this
who wouldn't yearn for love
alone and lonely
at the loom?

this lofty hall
with broken walls
on all four sides
lets wind-gusts in

if my flimsy skirt
should blow apart
promise to hide
that silly grin

green lotus
in clear water
flowers
fresh and red

my lover saw
and wanted one—
why not pluck
this flower instead?

you came to me
in midnight frost
and there was I
prepared to scold

embracing
in the icy dark
sudden sunshine
banished cold

spring flowers
enchant the woods
spring birds cry out
their yearnings from the trees

spring winds reply
with passion's zeal
my flimsy skirt
lifts in the breeze

now's the time
for blue-green banners
to celebrate
three months of spring

deep in the forest
magpies chatter
and everywhere
cicadas sing

wild winds ravish
blossom branches
a pale sun gleams
through waning mist

his thoughts led
to my chamber door
it's springtime—
how could I resist?

when she came to you
how could you refuse?
your fickleness
is hardly news

if you neglect this
open door, it droops
and won't fit
tightly as before

I'm still too young
to play along
with all your
devious ways

you're forever
like the duckweed
pulled here and there
with each spring breeze

a rocky region:
loving but resentful
I see winds
and cloud ahead

jade forest
stone tower
how can tender
words be said?

since you went away
what day goes by
when I don't
pine for love?

once autumn leaves
wither and fall
they can't fly back
to the branch above

I think of nothing
but our passion
since he turned
from love so early

a faint mist blurs
the lotus flowers
where once
I saw them clearly

I remember
days of spring
as autumn's
twilight nears

playing all those
games of love
we lost sight
of the passing years

walking in
the wild woods
desolate and bare
as human grief

sudden joy!
I burst out singing—
one casual flower
beneath a leaf

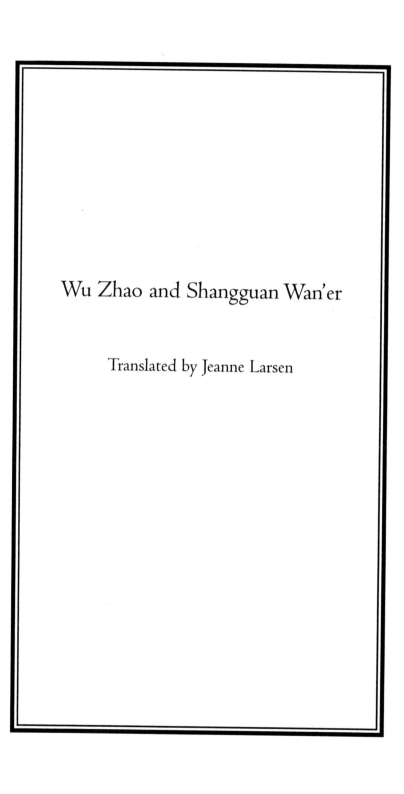

Wu Zhao and Shangguan Wan'er

Translated by Jeanne Larsen

The lives of these two remarkable women were, for forty years, intertwined. Both attained positions at court from which they could wield authority at a level denied most women—and most men—in the turbulently flowering first century of Tang China. Both made deft use of the rhetoric, symbols, rites, and expediencies of power. And for both, intelligence, learning, and the hard-won privilege of agency gave rise to an impressive gathering of poems, a few of which survive.

Wu Zhao (c. 625-705) was the only woman in Chinese history to hold the throne in her own right. She eventually founded a new dynasty, the Zhou, which lasted nearly fifteen years before the restoration of the Tang dynastic name. Earlier, she had for decades ruled de facto, first behind the throne and then beside it.

In her early teens, Wu joined the household of an emperor as a mid-ranked consort from an affluent family. In time, she attracted the notice of his son and after the father's death, entered the new emperor's household, at a higher rank. This was quite out of line with Confucian views of proper sexual behavior, though perhaps less shocking from the perspective of Inner Asian peoples with whom the Tang elite had considerable affinities. With this second husband, the emperor Li Zhi (known as Gaozong), Wu had children who would jockey for, and sometimes hold, the throne. But her voice and her administrative skills held sway during the last quarter-century of Gaozong's reign and the short reigns of two of her sons, one of whom was returned to sovereignty some ten months before the ailing octogenarian Wu Zhao died.

Stories of this capable woman's ruthlessness abound in the traditional histories. Certainly, she out-maneuvered three generations of female rivals within the palaces, as well as male courtiers and officials, and princes with their own imperial ambitions. We can only guess whether she used, or was used by, the men who were her favorites or lovers in the years of her widowhood. Wu was independent-minded, shrewd, and sometimes willing to listen to criticism. She employed means from slander to alliance, from murder to co-option, from adroit claims upon the moral high-ground to executions, secret police, and military force when rebellion flared.

The record of Wu's actions indicates that the feeling for her mother informing the poem translated here was strong. Wu Zhao was in her mid-forties when Lady Yang died; the daughter would have begun her study of poetry and Confucian ritual at this educated, devoutly Buddhist, woman's knee. As Empress Consort, Empress Dowager, and Empress Regnant, Wu Zhao supported Buddhism in many ways (along with Daoist practices and teachings, and Confucian scholars' work). This poem—with its theme of transience, its golden wheel evoking the ideal Buddhist monarch, its praise for the buddha Shakyamuni, and its reminders of the peace to be found in seclusion from secular life—suggests motivations more complex than political pragmatism alone.

Shangguan Wan'er (664-710) also rose to power on a treacherous path. She too flourished amid the intrigues and factions of court, but finally fell foul of them. Wu Zhao was around forty when Shangguan Wan'er's aristocratic father and grandfather—no friends to Wu—met death as punishment for an alleged plot against Wu's husband Gaozong. The infant Wan'er and her well-educated mother wound up in servitude in the imperial palaces. The talented girl was in her early teens when Wu, having heard of her literary brilliance, tested it. Shangguan Wan'er became personal secretary to the Empress Consort, and ultimately, a high-ranking consort to Wu Zhao's son and successor, Li Xian (known as Zhongzong). Although she fell temporarily out of favor with Wu at least once, and was nearly put to death, Shangguan flourished under both monarchs. Over the years, she authored imperial edicts, screened position papers from government ministers, judged literary competitions at court, and did important administrative work outside the official structure. Her actual poetic oeuvre included poems ghostwritten for Zhongzong and a number of imperial women.

In poems to her husband, we see Shangguan's skill with learned allusions that subtly exhort this sometimes careless and extravagant monarch—although she herself has been accused of financial excess in support of poetry gatherings and Buddhist institutions. Many of the poems here celebrate an outing from the capital to the country estate of one of the princesses of the blood who, along with Wu Zhao and Zhongzong's tough-minded chief wife, Empress Wei, often played major roles in the factional politics of the time.

Shangguan Wan'er survived Wu's fall and demise, and the fierce intrigues thereafter. A month after Zhongzong's death, however, the prince who was to rule as "the Brilliant Emperor" of the Tang's golden era engineered a coup. Shangguan's verbal skills could not save her and, like the other influential women at court, she was killed. It was this same man who ordered the compilation of her poems.

J L

Wu Zhao

To Shaolin Temple in His Majesty's Carriage,
After my Mother's Death

The trappings ring as we ride out
       through gardens his alone. I've left
my untouched rooms to wait upon his pleasure.
       A cloth of cloud drapes along the peaks.
Sunset drops, and through its streamers
       the hills' waves rise. From sun's palace,
we're announced to creekside shacks.
       Moonlight will post word on cave-house doors.
A wheel of gold—turned, and the land's
       gold too. Down corridors incense-scented,
robes of incense glide. Great bell, sutra-chanting:
       each sounds in its own light way.
Temple banners waver. Thin mists flurry.
       Once, a wildfire burned away
the seers' medicinals. These slopes went red.
       From field to field it flew. The flowery
upland meadows? Not half a shadow's left.
       Yet Lotus Pagoda keeps its glory, whole.
If you give yourself over
       to Shakyamuni's strength, you're part
of the perfection of this world;
       compassion's karmic threads spin out
a better life. What I want here
       is to take refuge, shave my head.
But a windblown branch has no way
       to find peace. Weep till you bleed, and still,
what's lost is lost.

Shangguan Wan'er

Silk Flowers at a Banquet in the Women's Palace on Spring's First Day: Written to Rhyme with Others' Poems, on Imperial Command

it's because   they're snipped
& stitched   that these clustered
petals burst   forth.   new
blossoms   that unfurl   only
after   they've been cut.
take up a branch: no, you
can't really   call *faux*   false.
but pick one bloom &   (how can
this be?)   see   nothing
at its heart.   spring's
here so they've   appeared   yet
never once   when fall returns
have such consented   to depart.
let me ask   the flowering peach
& early plum: come your dizzy
mingling   flurries
what   will happen   then?

Three Poems Presented Upon an Imperial Visit to Xin Feng
& the Palace at Hot Springs

    winter's deepest   month in this
    His Majesty's new era: his escort countless
    carriages   he leads us   out
    past Ba River to view   these scenes.

    gaze far & long   where bright bolts   leap
    as dragons   for horses   serve.
    turn back   regard   the frosted plain
    its fields all   whitest jade.

imperial phoenix flags   stream out.
they brush   the sky &
swirl.   mounted archers & chariots swift
as Shadow-Treader's galloping
come   forth.

Li Mountain flicks in &   out
of sight   stretching   beyond
the clouds. distant   distant
a canopy   spreads: His Majesty's
& on the very   level   of the sun.

tent-screens trimmed with kingfishers'
flash   & pearl-sewn hanging blinds:
in the moonlight   camp's laid out
fine bronze bowls   & jade ewers   brim
afloat   with pure orchid wine.

if season   after season   & year
upon year   we could go
unwavering on   in His Majesty's train
then in happy peace   we'd flourish
for as long   as *long*   is *long*.

from *Twenty-Five Poems upon Traveling to the Changning Princess's Floating Wine Cup Pond*

I.

chasing after   what gods treasure
open to   deep quietude
leap beyond   Elysian ranges
cross far   archipelagos

5.

branches, twigs   thick-thriving, lush:
design & substance   well refined
in company   of hillside groves
moon-trees, pines   shall grace, stand guard

7.

not one word about holy Round-crag
enough on Square-pot that faerie isle
what castle like Old Undefeated?
just this, divinities' glittering home

8.

the moon   that ring
of whitest jade   soars over
what's been built in this
far place.   the villa's walls
metallic-bright   do bear
uncommon   glory.   yet
best not play around with
trinkets   trimmed in pearls & gems
but keep to wisdom's   feel
for rivers   a kind heart's
love   of hills.   this grotto
was dug   for a refuge.   live trees
were counted on   to form
these   colonnades.   antiquity's
great artisans,   inventor
of chisel & plane,   now   this
exists   must hide away
their buried fame.

10.

dawn   clouds gone now.
airs clear   April-soft.
we   open up
our jackets' necks   think
with awe of mystics   vines
wrapped round their waists.   this
tortoise-shell: how it   seems
to hold   spring's dappled
look   in ice.   that porcelain
shivering   floats along
the rippled   waters.
sit on a stone   legs dangling
loose spirit-summoning   shrills.
or climb a pine &   all
at once let   brief lyrics
burst.   who   save those who've
left   the world of forms behind
can come here?   who
would pass   on through?

13.

leaning on   her hiking stick
she looks at summits   gone
sunrise-red.   her steps
precarious   walks
down   on the frost-touched
trail.   what   she wants
is to take off after
a stillness   of unplumbed
hills   her path   to follow
the cove-creek's   curves
to lose her   way.
in time she awakes   to ease
of spirit   of mind   & in one
flash sees   fog   sees clouds
all drop away.   don't think
her strange   the woman
who scrawls this
on a tree.   it's only
what comes   of being
in this mountain-deep
place   of rest.

14.

clutching at creepers   calling for
The One Gone Far
then stretched out under   moon
trees   yes   that's right
for this mountain-deep   mood.
there   on the creek
watch what   looks   like trees.
within   the wind
make out those   sounds
a sound   of pines.

17.

drop-offs   ravines   but no
holding back   we climbed
to look out   look down
eyes   made bright   hearts
joyful again   set in harmony.
grove   of bamboo   wind
blown   brings   long flutes
to mind.   currents in
the creek play   what
could be   a dulcimer's call.

20.

water falls   down rock-face   & clear
skies seem to rain.   bamboo's
dense stands   make   bright day
into dusk.   here in these hills
leisure   & pleasure.   so
begging your leave   we'll
send word   to that prince
who would live   in   the wild.

25.

we took to the heights   gazed
down   sheer drops   set
our hearts to rights.   we have
no time   to seek   fantastic
mushroom-palace spires   lost
shangri-las.   lingering snow
covers   woods transformed
to white stone trees.   what ice
storm left   touches hilltops   now
tors of pure jade   colorless.

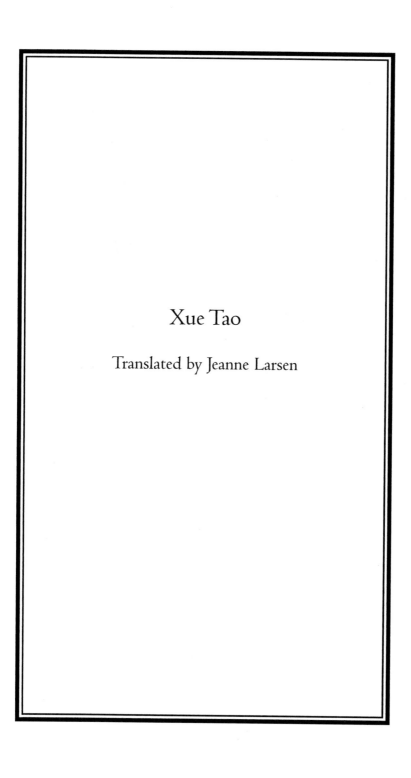

Xue Tao

Translated by Jeanne Larsen

Xue Tao (c. 768-831), who used the literary name "Hongdu," won high regard during her lifetime for her skillful, varied poetry. A substantial fraction of her work has been preserved; the majority is lost. Many twentieth-century sources give 768-831 or 832 as the years of her birth and death; research in China in the past two decades favors birth in 770 or even 781.

The leading male writers of her day exchanged poems with Xue. Tradition records her family's origins in the Tang capital, Chang'an (modern Xi'an), her father's early death, and her official registration as a courtesan. She flourished as a hostess-entertainer attached to the government of much of modern Sichuan province, headquartered in Chengdu. A survivor of political turmoil and military invasion, Xue became known for her wit and her skill as a calligrapher. In mid-life, she adopted Taoist garb, signaling her assumption of one of the few alternative life-roles available to women, and retired to a home just west of Chengdu, on the Wanhua River, in a district known for the crafting of high-quality paper, and perhaps not coincidentally for having been the residence of the great male poet Du Fu a generation before. Her figure has attracted colorful stories as well as a few doubtful poem-attributions—and her talent, the admiration it well deserves.

J L

Seeing-Off Associate Secretary Yao

Early fall and the river willows'
thousand-stranded withes

bend down lithe,
wave up in the wind,
their color
not yet gone.

"Willow" means "stay":
I'll break one off
for your farewell gift.

Do not let this
moonlit haze
know the sorrow of
two towns.

Homethoughts

At the foot of Mothbrow Mountain,
the river:
glossy, slick.

It grieves me
that our two hearts match
and yet your boat's not moored.

When will a slip of sail
leave the Brocade City's banks,

as we sing together
to the sound of oars
and set out
in midstream?

Willow Floss

Early March: willow catkins
light and fancy-free.

The spring breeze makes them weave
and waver
and tease people's clothes.

The girls in that house?
They are, at root,
unfeeling things.

Once committed to flying south
they're off and flying—
north.

A Wandering Tour of the Countryside in Spring: Sent to Master Sun

Head bent, I stood long
before a rambling rose,

lovely as fragrant basil:
its scent clung to my skirts.

Master Sun of Jadegreen Stream,
explain it all to me—

those shrikes
departing from the east,
those swallows, flying west.

Sent upon Being Ill and Unable to Accompany
Minister Duan on an Excursion to Wudan Temple

Wasted away: no longer
fit for audience with milord.

No use for falling flowers
to resent east winds
that bring them down.

Though I still say my heart
holds the green of spring,

what shame if my hair were reflected
in "Stone Mirror" on Wudan Hill,
bedraggled as tumbleweed!

Trying on New-Made Clothes

The Nine Humors split and woven
into nine-colored clouds of dawn,

the Five Magic Beasts reined in
to pull
a five-cloud chariot:

east wind blowing past
the palace of Spring's Lord

stole these designs for
human realms
to dye a hundred flowers.

For Someone Far Away

Flexible, frail
new willow leaves
once more in even ranks.

Deep in spring, catkins
falling
clog
the tree-lined creek.

I know that you still guard
Qin Pass in the far northwest.

Moonlight shines on a thousand doors:
I hide my face in
my arms.

Another Poem for Minister Wu on Arriving at the Borderlands

Pull up!
At Pull-the-Reins-Up Ridge
cold, and colder still.

The fine drizzle, the gentle breezes
pierce my liver and heart.

Just let me go back
to my place in town;

I swear I'll never even look
at landscapes
painted on screens.

On Beyond-the-Clouds Temple

I have heard of the moss
at Beyond-the-Clouds:

where winds blow high,
where sun is near,
it's free of the finest dust.

When level cloudbanks splash
their dye
on the Lotus Wall,

it seems to wait for a poet
and for the jewel moon.

Written on Lord-Bamboo Shrine

Before Lord-Bamboo Shrine:
how many ancient trees!

When sun at evening
slips away,
the hills go greener still.

From what village
by what stream
do bamboo flutes ring out?

Singing, singing: each
sound a song
welcoming the lord.

On Visiting the Shrine at Shamanka Mountain

Where gibbons howl
distraught and wild,
I visit Highpath Shrine.

The trail goes into sunset mists—
scents of herbs and trees.

The mountain's vivid beauty:
still
can't forget that poet.

The sound of waters:
crying yet
for King Xiang,
bereft.

Dawn after dawn
night after night
down beneath Yang Ledge,

making clouds and making
rain,
and Chu, his kingdom, lost.

Forlorn and mournful
before the shrine:
so many willow trees

dispute the length
of their green-painted brows
in vain
when springtime comes.

Water Chestnut and Salad-Rush Pond

Salad-rushes
droop, meandering
where the green cress floats.

Willow floss and
mingling leaves
couch upon clear currents.

When shall we near the headwaters
and admire these things,

whirled back to pluck the chestnut blooms,
whirled back
in drifting boats?

Sending Old Poems to Yuan Zhen

The urge to make poems:
everyone's got it.

But I alone
really grasp
rich subtleties of scenes.

I sing of flowers beneath the moon,
loving what's still and pale,

or write of willows at rainy dawn
for sake of their angled fringe.

Women like Green Jade
have long been kept
hidden in secret depths.

And yet, I always write
as I please,
on my scarlet poem-slips.

Grown old, one can't collect one's work
and fix up all that's wrong.

So I send these poems to you,
as if shown to teach a boy.

Yu Xuanji

Translated by
Geoffrey Waters and Jeanne Larsen

NOTE: The translations by the late Geoffrey Waters and his introduction have been edited for inclusion in this book.

MEF

Even though details of her life are fragmentary, Yu Xuanji's (844-c. 871) poems are of immense value as a mirror of her life and times; they also happen to be individual creations of haunting beauty, expressing her life experiences in language that is unusually direct and spontaneous.

Sources for Yu Xuanji's life are relatively meager, and of questionable accuracy: a lurid tale written a few years after her death, a handful of mentions in literary essays over the next few centuries, and a short biography in a standard "Lives of the Poets" finished in 1304. She also left us clues in her fifty or so surviving poems. If we examine this modest material, an outline of her life emerges.

Yu Xuanji was born around 844. She grew up in the entertainment district of the Tang capital Changan. In the course of her duties as a courtesan, she met a young scholar named Li Yi (Li Zian) who was in Changan to prepare for the Imperial Examinations. He passed the examinations in 858, earning the prestigious degree Presented Scholar. That year, when she was probably fourteen, she became his concubine. Li eventually took Yu Xuanji home to Zezhou, the present-day Jincheng in Shanxi. The traditional story tells us that Li Yi's principal wife was jealous and eventually forced him to get rid of her; when in 860, Li Yi was posted to Yuezhou in present-day Hunan, Yu Xuanji was no longer with the family.

In the next few years Yu lived as a courtesan in the area around Wuchang, on the Yangzi River. Eventually, she made her way back to Changan, where she took up residence as a Daoist nun in the Xian Yi Temple. At this time she was probably still under twenty years old. Among her patrons, friends and admirers during this period were famous poets, including the libertine Wen Tingyun and the scholar-official Li Ying, with whom she exchanged poems.

A Daoist temple was one of the few places where women could conduct their lives on an equal footing with men. In contrast to the Confucian moral code, Daoists did not regard sexual freedom as incompatible with their beliefs. Indeed, some of the rituals involved sexual intercourse between participants. Courtesans were frequently attracted to temple life as an escape from the greater constraints of life outside.

In a document called "Notes from the Three Rivers," a collection of anecdotes from Changan of that period, written by Yu Xuanji's contemporary, Huangfu Mei, there is a lurid story describing the circumstances of her death. He maintains that Yu had a beautiful young maid named Green Pearl, of whom she was jealous. Yu quarreled with Green Pearl over a relationship with a certain gentleman caller. Accusing Green Pearl of treachery, Yu allegedly beat her to death with a cane and buried the body in her back garden. The body was soon discovered, and despite pleas for clemency from influential friends such as Wen Tingyun and the Metropolitan Governor Wen Zhang, Yu was sentenced to death and executed.

We will never know how much of Huangfu Mei's story is true, especially the more sensational parts. It is hard to believe that the woman who wrote these poems could have committed such a vicious crime for such a petty motive. Given the atmosphere of intrigue predominant at that time, the charge could have been false, generated by a rival or someone with a revenge motive.

In her brief life as a concubine, a courtesan and a Daoist nun, Yu Xuanji clearly had a wide experience of men and formed complex relationships, by no means all of them sexual. The variable climate of these relationships is celebrated in her poetry, often in the form of letters addressed to lovers or friends. In many poems, as with other poets of the time, the natural scene is evoked and intimately connected to her emotions and reflections on life.

G W

Translations by Geoffrey Waters:

Poem on the Theme "Riverbank Willows"

Kingfisher blue along a tangled bank;
Mist gathers at a far tower.

Shadows creep across autumn water.
Flowers fall around fisherman's heads.

Fish hide in old roots;
Twigs catch on travelers' boats.

The wind's whistle on a rainy night
Invades my dream. I awake to grief.

I Was Expecting a Friend, But He Was Held Up by Rain and Didn't Come

Wasted faith in fish and geese,
The welcome feast laid out in vain.

My locked gate traps the moonlight.
I raise the screen to watch approaching rain.

A near spring laps stone steps.
Far waves caress the shore.

Thoughts of home, fall sadness;
I sing our song again.

To the Daoist Master

Sunset colors, cut and sewn in robes.
Incense through embroidered curtains.

Lotus petals flying everywhere.
Spare landscapes woven in my gown.

Stop on the path, hear the orioles;
Open the cage, let fly this crane.

In the high hall, rousing from a spring dream.
Now at evening: driving rain.

Selling Ruined Peonies

Sigh in the wind fall flowers, petals dance,
Their secret fragrance fades; it's yet another spring.

Too costly, no one bought them;
Too sweet for butterflies.

If these red blooms had flourished in a palace,
Would they now be stained by dew and dust?

If they grew now in a forbidden garden,
Princes would covet what they could not buy.

Emotions at the End of Spring, Sent to a Friend

Orioles chattering ruin my dream.
Carelessly I brush away the tears.

New moon, thin through dark bamboos;
Evening mist thick above the quiet river.

Nesting swallows carry mud.
Bees fly home with fragrant harvest.

Sad solitude, thoughts that never end;
Sing no more of pines with drooping branches.

Rhyming with my New Neighbor to the West, Hoping He Will Ask Me Over for Some Wine

When a poem comes, I hum it a hundred times,
New feelings word by word with golden sound.

I look west and long to climb the wall.
What, beyond, would melt my frozen heart?

River of Stars empty at the time agreed;
Ruined dreams of Xiao and Xiang, the lute foresworn.

When cold weather comes, I think of home.
How can you pour out purest gold alone?

Spring Thoughts Sent to Zian

The mountain road is steep, stone steps are dangerous;
The hard climb hurts me less than thoughts of you.

Ice melts in a far stream: sad music of your voice.
Jade snow on cold peaks: a memory of you.

Don't listen to the singers, springsick with wine.
Don't call your guests at night for games of chess.

Our promise endures like pine or stone,
So I can wait for wings to pair.

I walk alone at the cold end of winter.
Perhaps we'll meet when the moon is round.

What can I give my absent man?
In the pure light, tears fall: a poem.

To the Scholar Ren, Who Endowed the Zifu Temple

The hermit made a sacred place;
Pilgrims stop to see.

Donors' names on a dusty wall.
No name yet for the lotus hall.

Dig a pool, the water rises.
Open a path, green grass returns.

One hundred feet of gold, the turret burns:
Bright eye above the river.

Telling My Feelings

Sad music from vermilion strings.
How can I embrace it?

Early I knew the lover's touch,
Before I found refinement.

Gleaming, gleaming the peach and plum:
What harm if scholars seek them?

Green, green the pine and cinnamon:
The world respects them.

Clear moon on mossy steps,
Deep in the bamboo yard, a song.

Outside the gate, red leaves on the ground.
Wait for him. Why sweep them now?

To Wen Tingyun

Startled crickets call near stony steps.
Pure mist and dew on courtyard branches.

In this moonlight, I hear a neighbor's song.
From this tower, distant hills begin to glow.

Cool breeze over precious mats,
Remorse rises from an inlaid lute.

My friend is lazy, never writes.
What cure for this autumn mood?

Letting My Feelings Out

Idle and relaxed,
Alone with wind and light.

Clouds break, moon on water,
Adrift and free in a boat.

Sounds of a lute from a Buddhist temple.
A poem chanted in some splendid hall.

Clumps of bamboo my companions;
Stones my friends.

Swallows and sparrows follow me;
I need no silver, no gold.

Fill the cup with green spring wine.
Under the moon, subtle music.

By the clear pond around my steps
I tug at my hairpin, let the bright stream flow.

In bed reading,
Half-drunk, I get up to comb my hair.

Parting

Water yields; impossible to hold.
Heartless clouds fly off; will they return?

Sorrow in a windy spring; sunset over Chu River.
A single duck flies by, hunting its lost flock.

For My Friend Orchid

Morning and evening, drunk and singing,
Again this spring, I think of you.

Sad inside my window,
I look for a messenger in the rain,

Roll the pearl screen to see the mountains;
Views of fragrant grass begin new sorrow.

Since we parted at the feast,
How many times have you charmed them all again?

Playing Polo

Hard, round, clean, smooth: a shooting star.
Moon-sticks vie to hit it, never resting.

When you're free, whack it!
When you're blocked, hook it!

Don't give up, it's close at hand;
If you're scared, you'll never win.

At last, a goal, and that's the end:
You've won the finest prize my friend!

Regretful Thoughts

Fallen leaves scattered by evening rain;
Singing and strumming red strings alone.

Stay unmoved by heartless friends;
Stand firm, cast suffering to the waves.

Outside the gate pass carriages of the gentry.
Daoist books are tumbled on my pillow.

Dressed in cotton comes a guest of cloud.
Clear water, blue hills: those days are gone.

Staying in the Mountains in Summer

I've moved to the place of Immortals;
Flowers everywhere, no one planted them.

My clothes are hung to dry on a courtyard tree.
Sitting by a fresh spring; floods of wine.

The balcony merges into deep bamboo.
Books and silks are cast aside in heaps.

Idle in a painted boat, I sing to the moon,
Trusting in the breeze to blow me home.

Metaphor

Red peach flowers everywhere; springtime,
Green willows in each courtyard; moonlight.

Newly adorned, in a night tower vigil,
Sitting in my boudoir, alone with my emotions.

Fish play beneath lotus leaves;
Sparrows call from a far-off rainbow.

In this world, grief and joy jostle for our dreams,
How can we embrace them both?

Translations by Jeanne Larsen

Grief in an Inner Room

herbs with the scent
of a love now gone
fill my hands. in this slanting
light I tear up as I hear:
the man next door's come home.

on the same day you
set out, wild geese
left the southland, flying
north. this morning
Siberian flocks head south.

spring comes. fall
goes. thoughts of you
remain. fall goes and
spring comes back.
you don't send much word.

the doorbar's dropped. none make it
through my scarlet gate.
what does it serve, the pulsing
sound of fullers' rods,
slid in past my bed-drapes' gauze?

Winter Night

(for Wen Feiqing, a.k.a. Wen Tingyun)

painful thoughts. the search
for a poem. by lamplight, saying
lines out loud.

not sleeping makes
night longer. I dread my cold quilt.

garden covered
with leaves. sad that
the wind's come up.

sheer curtains.
window-screens of silk.
loving and mourning
the way moon sinks.

divided. distanced. ease
hasn't come.
in the end, I'll do what I want.

all that rises and falls is
empty, I see that—
with my original mind.

coming to rest in solitude.
never settling on a home:

all evening, sparrows
chittered, circling
the woods. to what end?

Poem to Echo One You Sent

(for a friend)

what does it take
to melt away
the despair of living on the road?

red slips of paper unfolded, I saw
the fine strokes of your hand:

showers that spatter
Paradise Peak, a thousand more hills
made small,

winds that flute through Bamboo Gorge
as autumn comes to innumerable leaves.

I went over your words this morning,
one by one:
worth more than emerald jade.

tonight, beneath
the quilts, I'll read them
aloud, again,
again.

a cedar chest will hold them safe.
but first, for a little longer
I keep them near.
I chant. they ring.

Written in a Pavilion Lost in the Mists

spring flowers, fall's
full moon:
      the stuff of poems.

cloudless sun. clear
nights. here: mountain
      spirits, loosed.

no reason I raised
the pearl-sewn blinds.
      won't lower them.

my couch is moved for good now.
I'll turn toward these hills
      and sleep.

As Autumn Begins

chrysanthemum buds
harbor fresh colors.
hills stretch far off in this evening's mist.

the chill wind startles green trees.
fall's clear notes
take these red silk strings.

a woman who can't stop thinking,
cloth on her loom: a man
deployed under foreign skies.

geese can fly.
fish move with the rivers.
a letter—but how would that get through?

A Few Notes at the End of Spring

shabby house at a small street's end.
not much company.
a long-ago lover stays with me
in my dreams.

perfumes blow in: silken clothes
at someone's party. the wind
carries songs from a fancy house.
I don't know where.

the main road's close. drumbeats roared,
marching through my morning sleep.
garden's quiet—till magpies'
luk-luk-luk!
disturbs this spring tristesse.

how could I keep chasing after
human things?
my life's a boat
that slipped its mooring,
more miles ago than I can count.

For Zian, Across the Han River

north of the river,
    south of the river,
        I look long. despair.

thinking of you.
    no, obsessed with you. and
        reciting poems. but why?

duck and drake
    lie warm together
        on sandy shoals.

through tangerine groves,
    lovebirds, purple,
        fly at their ease.

muffled by mists,
    voices in song
        and hidden away.

the ferry dock,
    its colors drained,
        submerged in moony light.

feeling fills me:
    only yards away
        or call it, ten thousand miles.

and then, then I hear,
    from house after house
        old love-songs' rhythmic sounds.

Lines Written in Depression at Little Jiang-Ling

(for Zian)

maple leaves—a thousand
boughs. no, more
than you could count.

the bridges, their rivery
images, hidden.
evening's sails move slow.

like waters
out of the west, these heartfelt
thoughts of you rush on:

all day, eastward and unceasing,
nights too, ceaseless, off to the east.

Poem Mailed to Zian

a little drunk
when we said good-bye.
but a thousand bottles
can't wash this sadness out.

at parting, my belly: a hundred knots.
no way to untie them.

your Sweet Orchid fades.
she's going back
to gardens where young men's
fancies turn,

where willows keep company
with passing ships,
till they move
on somewhere. west.
or east.

getting together, going
our ways. I've already
grieved—can't
count on clouds.

this hung-up love needs
to learn from the river: it keeps
on going on.

yes, there's a season
when flowers bloom. tough
to get there, I know.
and tough to connect.

yet I'm just not willing
to fill myself up
with drink
after drink, in some pretty white tower.

Farewell Poem

it was—how
     many?—nights' sweet
satisfaction in Flute Duet Tower.

a lover like a mountain
     god, who all
at once, took off.

asleep, then
     awake: never to speak
of where the clouds went.

one lamp burning
     low. fluttering, this
wild moth.

Breaking Off a Willow Branch for a Farewell Gift

another morning. another someone
leaves. tears ornament my hair.

spring blows through a mist
of willows, ragged
with all this breaking off.

I wish the western hills were bare of trees—

then nothing could cause this weeping,
this draping haze.

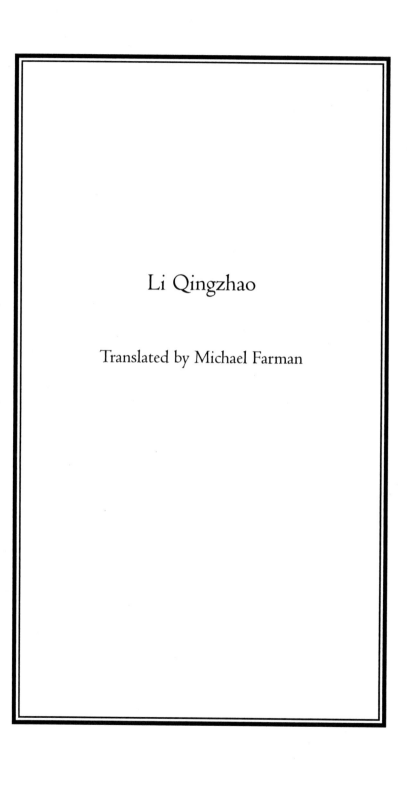

Li Qingzhao

Translated by Michael Farman

Li Qingzhao (1084–c.1150), China's most celebrated woman poet, was born into a privileged family of scholar officials. Her father was a professor at the Imperial Academy in the capital Kaifeng and a member of the literary circle which included the famous poet Su Shi (Su Dongpo). Her mother also came from a literary family and was an accomplished poet. Li Qingzhao, unlike most women of the period, was exposed from an early age to literature, music and painting, and encouraged to develop her literary and artistic skills.

In 1101, Li Qingzhao was married to Zhao Mingcheng, the son of another prominent politician. The pair shared a passionate enthusiasm for all the arts and spent most of their earnings gathering a collection of artifacts which included paintings, manuscripts, bronze vessels, stone rubbings and seals. This slowly grew into one of the most impressive collections in the country. They cataloged these items in a publication entitled *Jin Shi Lu* (*Records of Bronze and Stone*). In an epilogue, Li vividly described the pleasure they had from poring over these treasures and tells of the guessing games they played over provenances.

There were, however, severe political tensions that impinged on their family life; their existence was far from idyllic. The relentless power struggle in the Song Court between the social reformist faction led by Wang Anshi and the traditionalists, of whom Su Shi was a supporter, aligned the couple's politically powerful fathers into opposite camps. Over the next twenty-five years both families experienced the ups and downs of political disgrace and reinstatement as the influence of the two factions fluctuated. Then, in 1126-27, came the greatest catastrophe; the Jurchen people from the area now known as Manchuria invaded and eventually conquered the whole of China north of the Yangtse River, establishing the Jin Dynasty and forcing the Song Emperor and his court to flee south, where the city of Hangzhou eventually became the Southern Song capital.

Li and Zhao, like so many others, were forced to make the difficult journey south, taking whatever books and artifacts they could carry, but leaving the bulk of their collection behind to be plundered by the Jurchen. The couple moved to Nanking, where Zhao was appointed city magistrate. In 1129 he was suddenly taken ill and died soon after. Li was then forty-six years old.

Little is known about Li's life after her husband's death, although she continued writing poetry that was widely admired. In spite of the lack of real historic information, her predominant state of mind, and even biographical details, have been inferred by some commentators and translators simply from the evidence of her lyrics. This approach interprets her poems as direct personal expression, but to read them this way ignores the true nature of the poetic genre in which she wrote. The *ci*, or song lyric, is a carefully constructed artifice with a long history by Li's time, and embodied many conventions. A predominant convention was to use the persona of a woman left alone and sorrowful, longing for the male figure to return. It should be no surprise that this image was originally conceived by male poets, but Li and other women poets faithfully followed this convention.

If Li Qingzhao has lately become something of a feminist heroine, it is not because of the subject-matter of her poems, but because she was an outstanding poet at a time when this was considered to be a male preserve. To the extent that her own life paralleled the *ci* conventions, Li was able to channel her personal emotions into this highly stylized form and, through the freshness and inventiveness of her imagery, achieve something more universal. But the evidence we have of her ability to deal with the ups and downs in her eventful life, and the content of some of her other writings, reveal a remarkably determined and resilient personality very different from the persona of many of her poems.

It appears that she moved from city to city until she finally settled in Hangzhou in 1132. During her travels, she managed to preserve some of the depleted remains of her prized collection. Some later historical sources tell us that she married again, but that her new husband abused her and she divorced him after a few months, spending a brief spell in prison as a result. However, this information is unreliable; it may have been invented by political enemies in an effort to discredit her. She is believed to have died in 1150 or 1151.

M E F

To the Tune: Partridge Sky

Cassia Flowers

Tranquil in light yellow,
soft and yielding,
so reticent
only fragrance lingers.

No need for garish green or red—
these are by nature the most refined.

The envy of plums,
the shame of chrysanthemums,
they crown the Autumn Festival.

Poets can be so unfeeling.
Why have they ignored them?

To the Tune: Graceful Concubine

I sense that plum blossoms are opening behind the pavilion.

Lovely, frail,
densely perfumed,
they're deep among the sandalwood
where snow is thinnest.

This year, I can't bear to search for them
as once we did, at evening,
far between clouds and water,
from the river pavilion
to the house of pleasure.

Clear days find me,
emerald blinds rolled,
leaning on the rail.

When he arrives I'll stir myself,
set out a brimming jar of wine.
The music of our song
will drift across the water
to the clouds' end.

This blossom branch
transplanted to the south
needs constant nurture—
don't linger in those western halls
listening to barbarian pipes.

To the Tune: The Lovely Nian Nu

Once more the courtyard's desolate
with slanting wind and drizzle;
my heavy door stays shut.

As Cold Food Festival approaches,
I love the graceful willow catkins
that brave this weather.

After struggling with wilful rhymes,
I'm resting, head in hand,
sobering, savoring idleness.

Wild geese bound for Huai
already left—
they won't be carrying
my thousand cares to you.

Here in this high chamber,
through days of springtime chill,
all blinds drawn,
I'm listless, leaning on the balustrade.

Cold quilt, fading incense
and a new dream:
I won't allow this grief
to weigh me down.

Fresh morning dew,
young shoots on the phoenix tree:
Spring's waking up,
sun rising,
mist clearing:
today may be a fine day after all!

To the Tune: Good Times Soon

Fallen petals
outside my window:
abandoned by the wind;
heaps of crimson in the snow.

Remember how apple blossoms
open on cue
to mark Spring's sorrow?

Wine and songs over,
jade goblets empty,
light from the lamp-jar
fades and flickers.

The dream ended,
how to endure this bitterness
and constant cries of the cuckoo?

To the Tune: Butterflies Flirting with Flowers

A long weary night,
a few bright thoughts.
Futile dreams of Changan:
a vision of the Changan road,
joy in spring's arousal;
gleam of moonlight-kindled blossoms.

Carelessly scattered cups and dishes,
fine wine, pungent plums,
someone to embrace.

Drunk now, with tears not smiles,
I pity us, grown old like Spring.

To the Tune: Small Hills

Spring's arrived at Changmen:
young spring grasses,
red plum blossoms,
some barely open, wrapped
in clouds of jade dust.

Reaching for a daybreak dream
my cup of Spring shattered.

Shadows of flowers
press heavy on my doorway;
careless curtains hang loose
inviting moons
at twilight.

Three time in two years
His Lordship has gone east.
Come back Lord
share this spring with me!

Changmen: Literally "Long Gate," an allusion to the lonely chamber of Empress
Chen of the Han Dynasty, abandoned by her Emperor.

To the Tune: Butterflies Flirting with Flowers

Warm rain,
cleansing wind,
begin to vanquish cold.

Eyes of willows,
cheeks of plums,
already feel the pulse of spring.

Who will share with me
wine-befuddled poetry?
This hairpin weighs me down,
tears melt my rouge.

Struggling with my gold-thread robe,
I lean on pillow hills.
The phoenix hairpin falls,
lost among those slopes.

Alone in misery's embrace
with no fine dreams,
far into the night:
snuff the candle flame.

To the Tune: Butterflies Flirting with Flowers

A Letter to my Sisters from the Inn of Prosperous Pleasure.

Tears soak my silk robe,
wash away my powder.

We sang four times
the farewell song of Sunlit Pass
loud enough to reach a thousand ears.

The mountain paths are long,
rivers bar the way.

Here at the inn, alone,
I listen to each raindrop fall.

Flustered by farewell heartache,
I forgot your parting gifts:
the customary wine and verse.

Send good news
with overhead wild geese.
Donglai is not so distant
as Penglai, after all.

Penglai is the legendary Island of the Immortals.

To the Tune: Lone Wild Goose

Rising at dawn
from cane bed with paper screens—
so many words,
no fine thoughts.

Fragrance gone
from the jade burner:
cold companion to my liquid mood.

His flute would sound
three times over
the "song of broken blossoms"
charged with spring emotions.

Light wind, scattered rain,
patters on the ground.
A sudden downfall
weeps a thousand tears.

The flute player's gone,
the jade tower's empty,
who is there soothe a wounded spirit?

Once a branch is broken,
in this world or heaven
not a soul can mend it.

To the Tune: Sands of the Washing Stream

Aroused by Spring, but indolent, combing my hair.
Evening breezes in the courtyard
set plum blossoms tumbling.
Light clouds come and go;
the moon plays hide and seek.

Lazy incense smoke
drifts from the jade duck burner.
Here, behind cherry tasseled curtains,
will magic rhino horn ward off the cold?

To the Tune: Sands of the Washing Stream

Not too deep
into heavy amber wine,
intoxication came
before the wine took hold.
A distant bell
sounded on the evening breeze.

Overwhelming camphor perfume
ended the dream.
My lucky golden hairpin slipped,
loosed my coil of hair.
I sobered, spent,
facing the candle's red bloom.

To the Tune: Sands of the Washing Stream

Spring's pale sunshine
comes and goes
on Cold Food Day.

The last thread of smoke
curls from the jade burner.

Dreaming over,
my hairpin's lost
beneath the pillow mountain.

Now's the time
sea swallows return,
people meet to gather herbs.

At the riverside
plum blossoms have already tumbled,
willows unveil their catkins.

Twilight brings a little rainfall,
finds me idling on the rain-damp swing.

To the Tune: Sands of the Washing Stream

Recovering from sickness
with tangled hair,
I lie and watch
through the window screen
a slim moon rising.
I simmer pods of cardamon
in place of tea.

Reclining on my pillow,
reading ancient poetry
restores me.
Outside
healing rain arrives;
elegant cassia flowers
bow towards me.

To the Tune: Sands of the Washing Stream (Extended Version)

Cassia Flowers

Crush you into countless scraps of gold,
cut your jasper leaves
seam after seam,
your spirit,
like that of noble Yan Fu,
shines through still.

How coarse
those heavy sprays of plum,
lilacs tangled into bitter knots.

Your sweet odor
shows no mercy,
piercing this sad heart
with far-off dreams.

Yan Fu was a highly respected scholar of the Jin Dynasty (256-420 CE).

To the Tune: Telling Inner Feelings

Night comes:
drunk, I undress late,
plums wilting on my broken spray.

Sobering,
sleep spoiled by wine,
my dream fades
and won't return.

Silence.
The moon, reluctant to leave,
hangs beyond the emerald curtain.

I caress my final blossom
pressing out the fragrance
and memories of times gone.

To the Tune: A Sprig of Plum Blossoms

Red lotus fragrance fades;
the jade mat gathers autumn.
Alone with my orchid boat
I undo my silk robe.
Will some dweller-in-the-clouds
bring me a love message?
Maybe when wild geese return
moonlight will flood my room again.

Blossoms fade and fall,
water flows on;
there's no stopping them.

One kind of yearning,
two sites for sorrow:
these hurts refuse to fade,
and only move from brow to heart.

To the Tune: A Reproach for my Lord

Breezes on the lake
spread ripples far and wide.
Already dusk of autumn—
few bright flowers,
little fragrance left.

Shining waters,
mountain views,
lovers
with so much left to say.

Lotus pods already ripe,
leaves grown old,
duckweed on the bank
bathed in dew.

Gulls and egrets
sleeping on the sand
have turned their heads away,
as if they too are grieving
that you must leave so soon.

To the Tune: Memories of a Flute-player on Phoenix Terrace

Incense cold in the lions-head burner,
quilt crumpled into red waves.
I rise, too indolent to comb my hair,
dust on my precious toilet case,
the sun already at the curtain rail.

Dreadful, the pain of separation
so much left unsaid.
Lately I've grown thin—
it's not the wine,
nor the gloom of autumn.

Enough!
This time you had to go—
that farewell song,
if sung a thousand times,
wouldn't have kept you here.

My thoughts followed you
from this mist-enfolded tower
to your distant Wuling Spring.
Only the water flowing by
knows how I stood and gazed
all day.

From this time on,
a new array
of griefs to bear.

To the Tune: Remembering the Girl from Qin

From this high pavilion
scattered hills, open plains.
A gleam of mist,
a gleam of mist.
Crows fly home to roost
the sunset horn sounds.

Incense fragrance turns bitter,
a sudden wind-gust.
Wutong leaves tumble,
wutong leaves tumble.
Autumn again,
alone again.

To the Tune: Drunk Under Blossom Shade

Light mist, heavy clouds,
a long, dismal day.
Incense gone from the golden beast.

Double Ninth again!
Midnight chill invades
jade pillow, silk drapes.

At the east fence, wine in hand,
golden twilight fading,
fragrance lingers on my sleeves.

I can't say I'm not beguiled,
but west winds lift the curtains,
and I'm more fragile than these yellow flowers.

Double Ninth: The ninth day of the ninth month, once considered a date of ill omen, in which chrysanthemum wine was traditionally consumed to ward off evil. It is now a holiday in which people typically celebrate outdoors to enjoy the last fine autumn weather.

To the Tune: Constant Pleasure

A golden sunset—
clouds in twilight harmony;
where is he?

Dense mist stains the willows;
a plaintive flute
plays the willow song.

How much spring warmth
will find its way here?
Fine weather for the Lantern Festival—
days without wind or rain.

When wine and poetry friends arrived
with fancy horse and carriage,
I thanked them but declined.

I remember good times
back in my old city:
free and easy in the women's quarters,
kingfisher feathers in our hair,
binding gilded garlands
in happy competition.

Frail, with graying temples now,
fearful of going out at night
unlike those far-off days,
I hide behind my curtains
listening to the talk and laughter.

To the Tune: Fisherman's Pride

In snow, already signs of spring:
the jade-smooth branches
of my courtyard winter plums adorned
with fragrant faces, half-exposed:
delicate, like tender maidens
emerging fresh from their baths.

Did heaven summon up this moonlight
simply to display them?
Let's revel, you and I,
in green wine from the golden beaker,
intoxication welcome;
this flower has no equal.

To the Tune: Fisherman's Pride

Cloud vapors, morning mists
blend with sky.
The star river turning—
a thousand sails dancing.

As in a dream, my spirit returned
to the heavenly palace:
I heard a great voice
asking with compassion
where was I bound?

I answered with a sigh:
the journey's long,
twilight closes in.
Once I fashioned poems—
people were moved
by some of those lines.

Borne by the wind,
the giant Roc bird soars
ninety thousand *li.*

Wind, don't stop!
Bear this fragile vessel
away to the celestial hills.

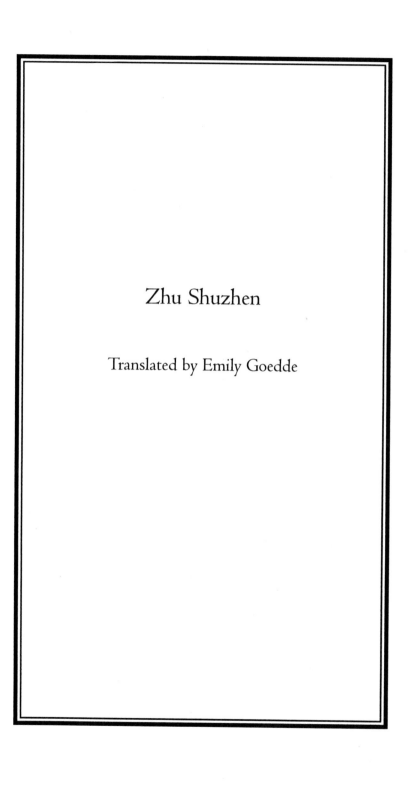

Zhu Shuzhen

Translated by Emily Goedde

Zhu Shuzhen has long been considered one of the most important female poets of pre-modern China, and her collected body of work, *Heartbreak* (*Duanchang shiji*) consists of over 300 poems. Nevertheless, we have no records of Zhu's date of birth or death, and scant information about her life; we cannot even say for sure whether she existed at all. The authorship of the poems credited to her has thus been the source of much debate. Were they written by a real person called Zhu Shuzhen, or were they partly or wholly written by someone else, even possibly a man?

The only evidence we possess today is all in the collection of Zhu's poems, furnished with a brief introduction by Wei Duanli, dated 1182. In the introduction, Wei claims that he discovered her poetry during a visit to Wulin, where he met people who were reciting poems that had been circulated by her friends. His introduction offers very little concrete information beyond stating that her parents were remiss in arranging an unsuitable marriage with "a common city dweller." It provides no exact dates for her birth or death.

Based on readings of his introduction and the poems themselves, some modern scholars have offered various dates and scenarios about Zhu's life. Dates for her life range from 1063-1106 to 1135-1180. Assumptions about her biography are based on the dubious practice of circular readings, whereby details in poems that are known to employ conventions and stylized imagery are nevertheless assumed to be autobiographical.

Despite doubts about Zhu's historicity and authorship, close familiarity with these texts convinces me that a woman named Zhu Shuzhen did write the bulk of the poems credited to her. I find in the poems a unity of voice. And I do not see in them the speculation of a male gaze, so frequently apparent in male-composed *ci* (or song lyrics). Nor do they seem overtly allegorical, voyeuristic or eroticized. For these reasons, I find it plausible that a woman named Zhu Shuzhen existed and wrote about the natural beauty that surrounded her as a means of engaging with the world.

To date, only small selections of translations of Zhu's work have appeared, mostly in large anthologies devoted to female poets. The translations included here are all selected from her *shi* (eight-line regulated verse) and *jueju* (quatrains) rather than her *ci*, although the latter are more commonly associated with the Song Dynasty and female poets, as there are more than 300 *shi* and *jueju* in her collection and only 33 *ci*.

In Wei Duanli's edition, the poems were organized into ten chapters based on seasonal themes, followed by chapters entitled "Chanting Praises" and "Boudoir Laments," the *ci* forming part of the last chapter. I have arranged this selection of the *shi* in the order that they are presented in the modern edition of her poetry *Zhu Shuzhen ji*, or *Zhu Shuzhen's Collected Works*, edited by Zhang Zhang and Huang Yuxiao.

One of the many difficulties facing translators of pre-modern Chinese poetry is the wide use of trope imagery, which often alludes to seasons and the emotions associated with them, or makes reference to lines of earlier poets, a practice that was considered an art in itself. Repeated imagery of this nature can seem hackneyed in contemporary English, partly because of different aesthetics, but also because we don't have the necessary cultural background to interpret the objects as invocations of states of mind or as poetic references.

EG

Balmy

Rain recedes from crabapple blossoms
in the deep courtyard
On windless, mossy paths
butterflies fly free
Clove blossoms
flaunt their beauty
Tamarinds
gently play
Early peach trees moist, satiny
pink, singularly pale
Foliage in the lingering cold
green slowly thickens
Still, silent behind pearl curtains
swallows not yet returned
Whenever the cuckoo cries
all of spring is saddened

Spring day poems

Spring has come, spring has gone
how many times?
This is not the year
of most regret
Crabapples still, silent
the moon above their boughs
shines on someone in the clear night
to what avail?

Lingering cold dissipates
in the day's mellow beauty
Spring stretches across plum blossoms
powders willow tops
Butterflies and bees know
how to satisfy new appetites
They spread their antennae, entering high
windows on busy wings

Opened blind, moon suspended
a slanting hook
When dusk comes, sadness
multiplies and grows
I sit alone at a small window
without companions
Shamefaced and numb
before crabapple blossoms

Moonlight sieved in latticework
a soft breeze rises
Weary eyes afflicted by spring
tears about to fall
I write and play *qin*
aimlessly
I haven't the heart
to go out spring green picking

Heavy mist, light rain
dampens petal dust
As if wanting to hide blackbirds
willows color anew
I can't remember how to play
the name-the-flower game
So rely on poems and wine
to banish spring

Since spring came
day after day sadness
Pity for flowers has turned
to shame on their behalf
Pair upon pair of swallows
twitter past
Annoyed, I let the curtains hang
unfastened from their hooks

Looking at flowers

I want to forget old troubles
to the flowers
But turn shy when
I face their muteness
However lovely,
spring must leave
Who will stay and keep
the lonely company?

Peach blossoms in full bloom west of my window

All this was sown
by Master Liu's hand
Since Master Liu's been gone
how many times they've bloomed
The sun, lord of the east,
will look after them
But heartless butterflies
don't visit anymore

Climbing a tower on an autumn day

Scattered shadows of parasol trees
play in evening light
Dying cicadas buzz cold, mournful
I can't bear to listen
From above, autumn mountains
to the end of my sight
Eyes brimming over
layer upon layer of green

Deep feelings on an autumn night

Crying wears out the eyes
completely breaks the heart
I fear after twilight
nightfall will come
Worse, I endure thin rain
on a new autumn night
A speck of dying lamp
to keep me company as the night grows long

Inspired by scenery

Half window, the entire setting sun
a curtain lifts in the breeze
Little, little pond, pavilion
a bamboo path
Maple leaves drunk red
in autumn color
Two or three rows of geese
centered against the evening sun

Mid-autumn downpour

Collected leaves
cold, flutter on the steps
Motionless clouds
obscure the sea's horizon
From above I
strain my eyes to see
The dimness of the sky
cuts off my heartsong
It keeps returning
sadness difficult to forget
A reunion time
not yet agreed
Around the four eaves
flies a driving rain
Inside, still, silent
I sit in this empty study

Sitting alone

I roll up the curtains
and wait for the bright moon
Rest my hand on the railing
and face the west wind
Night air
submerged in autumn color
Jeweled river
immersed in the deep blue void
Down in the grass
crickets sing
From the other side of the sky
geese call
So much has
happened
With whom
can I share tonight?

Melancholy: two poems

Rain falls, spills, soughs
dusk falls in the courtyard
Alone I face a solitary lamp
resentment high
Heartbroken, I
take up needlework listlessly
The wind's knife cuts leaf after leaf
from the parasol trees

Autumn rain falls with heavy drops
drip, drop all night long
Dreams won't come
I grow restless, lonely, cold
On banana leaves
in parasol trees,
dian dian sheng sheng—
the sounds of heartbreak

Gazing into the distance on the evening of an autumn day

In dense mist it's difficult to make out
hills of a different district
They resemble a flock of gulls
bathing on a far sandbank
A speck
of travelers' sail sways
Where rows of clouds and the red sun
play with the brilliant cold

Composing in the moonlight on a snowy night

An entire tree of plum blossoms
between the snow and the moon
Pure petals, moonwhite moon
and snow glow cold
Inside, outside
clear and pure
We serve wine, sing poems
and let inspiration rise without end

Imminent snow

Silent winter sparrows
fill bamboo thickets
Frozen clouds curtain the sky
snow about to fall
The north wind gives
no one special favors
Plum branches hold
their blossoms tight

Hearing blackbirds

Above the wall, beyond the flowers
discussing clear weather after rain
They disperse, distancing themselves from sadness
they're listening to something
The bluebird has received
cloud news
Before he finishes his duties, he reports
with a few cries

Written on the wall of Daoist woman Wang's hermitage

Low, low enclosure walls
little, little pavilion
Here and there, in the eaves,
jade echoes clear, cool
Dust flies but doesn't reach
someone always still
A single coil of incense
two rolls of scripture

Reading history

Historians' brushes gather
thousands of rhymes and reasons
Later generations encounter them
willfully blind
Confidently they distinguish
intentions and actions of kings and hegemons
But when it comes to doing something
that's always hard

Self-reproach: two poems

Women who dabble in literature
are certainly reproachable
I can't stand
"singing about the moon and humming about breezes"
"Wearing through iron ink-stones"
is not my business
Breaking golden needles in embroidery
now that's an accomplishment

When depression won't go away
I only read poems,
And again find
talk of separation
which adds to my longing
which turns to dejection
I understand now—being sharp
isn't as good as being dull

Humid night

Water, pavilion face each other
dusk now fallen
Many quiet fireflies fly
through the small garden
At the window a solitary lamp
flickers
Apathetic, alone
I'm too listless to bolt the door

Coming back late from a trip to the lake

I'm in love
with the scenery of the West Lake
Mountain peaks
carry the evening sun
Returning birds
flutter in bamboo dew
Falling fruit
echoes by the celery pond
Leaves rest
in the quiet of the breeze
Fish swim
in the cool of water's depths
A pavilion
half-lit, a moonlit scene
Lotus mist
inflames us with its perfume

On the lake, singing about the moon

Deep in the night the sky is clear
cool breezes rise
On the lake someone sings
"Strolling in the moonlight"
Water trickles and flows
shallow and clear
Moonwhite endless void
threads of mist evaporate
Water, light moonlight
two circles linked together
The moon, the moon's reflection
two sights unsurpassed

Searching for plum blossoms

Warm, soft weather
like mild spring
We search for winter plum blossoms
that already fill the hills
Laughing, I snap a sprig
tuck it into clouds of hair
And ask, "Is anyone
as elegant as this?"

New Year's Night

No need to sigh
constellations change
Look: spring
is about to return
Plates of spicy peppers
surround red candles
Cypress wine
brims over in golden cups
End of year candles
almost burnt out
New Year's
dawn watch is urged along
What is
earliest?
It could only be
the back garden plum blossoms

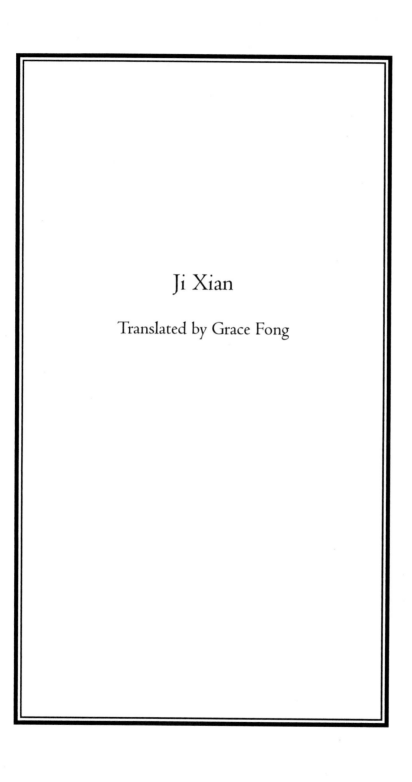

Ji Xian

Translated by Grace Fong

A native of Taixing County, Jiangsu province, Ji Xian (1614-1683) was born into a well-to-do scholar-official family in the affluent Yangzi Delta region. Her grandfather and father both served in high ministerial posts during the last decades of the Ming dynasty. Like her contemporary, the precocious but short-lived Ye Xiaoluan, Ji Xian was among the many talented girls who were given a literary education at home by her parents. In her middle age, after recovering from a chronic illness, she wrote an autobiographical essay entitled "Record of Past Karma," in which she revealed how she became a devoted Buddhist. When she was still a child of seven or eight, her grandmother took her to watch the Buddhist drama *Mulian Saves His Mother from Hell* at a temple fair. The experience awakened in her the desire to become a Buddhist nun. However, her parents had already betrothed her to the son of the equally eminent Li family in nearby Xinghua County. Like the majority of genteel women in late imperial China, Ji Xian had no choice but to accept the engagement and married Li Weizhang when she grew up. In every stage of her life, Ji Xian exerted herself to follow the Confucian models of exemplary feminine virtue, taking on the roles of filial daughter and daughter-in-law, caring sister, dutiful wife, and good mother. She taught her son and daughter how to read and write and compose poetry. Many poems in her collection, *Prose and Poetry from the Rain Fountain Shrine,* were addressed to them—to instruct, admonish, encourage, and comfort them, particularly to her son when he traveled to the capital to take the civil examinations. However, Ji Xian's spiritual yearning for a life of reclusion never subsided. She wrote many poems on the theme of living a simple life in the tranquility of nature, showing her mastery of the diction and imagery of recluse poetry, and at the same time imbuing it with a unique tension resulting from the social restrictions imposed on her gender. This religious longing was further fueled by her husband's growing philandering and her struggles to control her jealousy. Her autobiographical record ends with her initiating a move to a separate residence from her husband to pursue her Buddhist practice in peace.

G F

Composed at Random

The inkstone, a constant companion
Poems more than comfort poverty
A patched robe rids one of vulgar burdens
The bamboo couch stills the dusty clamor
I want to emulate the recluse at Mount Deer Gate
But being a wife, what can I do?
Turning to contemplate the delights of hills and streams
Awake or asleep I've long been close to them.

Evening Meditation

Season of yellow plum blossoms, fine rain, a sky of falling petals
Swallows twitter in front of embroidered curtains
Settled in meditation, unaware of dawn or dusk
A stone bed in bright moonlight, grass so luxuriant.

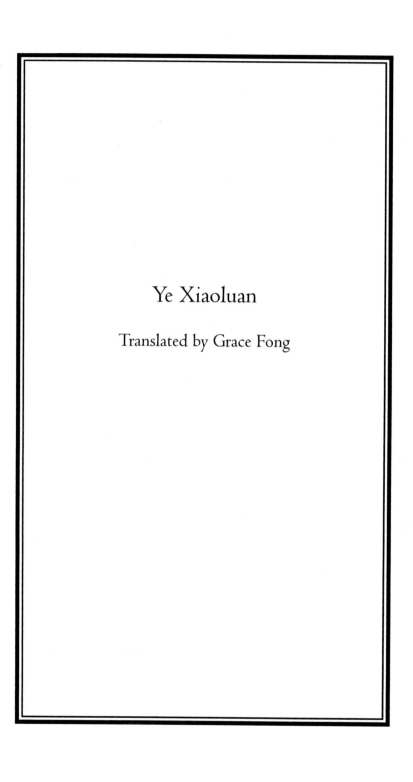

Ye Xiaoluan

Translated by Grace Fong

An astonishing rediscovery in the past two decades by literary scholars and historians of China is the vibrant literary culture among women of scholar-literati families in the Ming (1368-1644) and Qing (1644-1911) dynasties. Throughout early and medieval China, small numbers of educated women were recorded as having received a literary education, but, due to a confluence of economic and social trends and changing cultural practices, such as the boom in publishing, the increased circulation and availability of books, and the interest in educating daughters among the elite for a variety of reasons, the late sixteenth century witnessed the first blossoming of a women's culture based on literacy, especially in the affluent Yangzi River Delta region, which includes the present-day cities of Suzhou, Shanghai, Nanjing, and Hangzhou.

Ye Xiaoluan (1616-1632) was a native of Wujiang (now part of Suzhou). She was literally one among tens of thousands of young girls and women in her time who were taught how to read and write and compose poetry at home, usually by their mothers and fathers. Because of her short life and exceptional talents, Ye Xiaoluan quickly became a famous icon of the gifted young woman who suffered a tragic fate. Xiaoluan was the third daughter of Ye Shaoyuan (1589-1648) and Shen Yixiu (1590-1635), a companionable couple who gave birth to thirteen children. Shen Yixiu was herself an accomplished poet and writer, and her three elder daughters were all known for their literary skill. Because her cousin, Zhang Qianqian, was childless, when Xiaoluan was born, Yixiu gave her to her cousin to bring up. Xiaoluan therefore grew up under the care of her aunt Zhang Qianqian, who was also a woman with superb poetic gifts. When Xiaoluan returned to her parents around the age of ten after her aunt's early death, she was fully conversant with all the poetic forms, themes, and genres. Her posthumous collection of poetry, *Fragrance Returning to Life*, was compiled by her father. It contains ninety-five poems, ninety song lyrics, a Buddhist *gatha*, and two essays. Her poetry reflects the cultured life of a talented teenage girl, doted on by her parents and much loved by her siblings. The family often composed poems together using the same rhymes on festival days and family gatherings. When her father spent a year in the capital Beijing on official assignment, Xiaoluan sent him epistolary poems. She wrote poems on the happy occasions when her elder sisters came home to visit after they were married and wistful farewell poems when they left. Although her life was spent mostly in the inner quarters, Xiaoluan did go on excursions with her family to nearby scenic sites and wrote poems about them. In all, Xiaoluan's poetry exhibits an elegant balance between familiarity with the literary tradition and a lively imagination. Her poems often combine other-worldly Daoist imagery with an attitude of transcendence. As was customary, Ye Shaoyuan made an engagement for his daughter when she was still an infant. When Xiaoluan reached adolescence, he arranged for her marriage. However, Xiaoluan suddenly fell ill and died a few days before her wedding. She was barely sixteen. Her father read some of her poems as presaging her untimely death.

GF

To the Melody Immortal on the Bridge of Magpies

Inscribed on a Landscape Painting

A thatched gate left ajar
Misty green hills almost dripping
Reed flowers by a broken bank in a silent wind
Far-off peaks, trees in clouds, both hazy in the rain
A secluded path remote
Winding and hard to find.

An expanse of calm ripples
Tall pines standing in rows
Within reach—an immortal's couch in a jade grotto
Leisurely looking on and on, my thoughts roam faraway
How I wish my body could fly into the scene!

Excursion to West Lake, 1628

Willow catkins fly past the embankment
A sweep of dark green hills at dusk
Music and song carried away with the painted oars
Lingering on—the cool color of water.

On the Double Ninth, a Recent Composition

Wind and rain on the Double Ninth

Climbing up I mount the steps of a storied tower

Leaves of a courtyard pawlonia hasten to drop in the cold

Chrysanthemums by the hedge are thoroughly startled by autumn

Like Tao Qian with his flask of wine

I can't dispel the sadness of a thousand ages

Filling the sky—disordered reflections of clouds

And time flows away with the sound of wild geese.

To the Melody Partridge Sky

On a Spring Night in 1632, I Composed Five Lyrics in a Dream

I.

One scroll of the Lankavatara Sutra, one stick of incense

With a prayer mat my companion, I forget the world.

My spirit is not far from the three fairy isles in the emerald sea

A clear breeze blowing on half the pillow lengthens my dream.

Following the secluded path along a winding corridor

A thatched hut by a bamboo fence has the finest scene.

I just pity the swallows swooping back and forth—

Why busy yourselves building nests day after day?

II.

After a spring rain the hills turn a kingfisher green

A vine-covered gate opens towards the setting sun.

At dawn I go looking for magic fungus with my friends

At nightfall I return with a pitcher of wine.

I lean on a rock, hands holding a cup

When drunk who cares if the jade hills collapse?

Today we don't know what tomorrow will bring

If we don't get drunk, we would let time rush us in vain.

V.

I went west to visit the Queen Mother's Pool

Jasper Wine overflowed from goblets of rosy clouds in highest
    heaven

The sky was filled with stars—as if ready to be picked

Clouds and mists wrapped round my body like a robe

Riding on white deer, mounting green dragons

The immortals harmonized with my lyric Pacing the Void

As I took leave, Fairy Maid Double Completion offered a present—

Presenting me a five-colored magic fungus on a golden stalk.

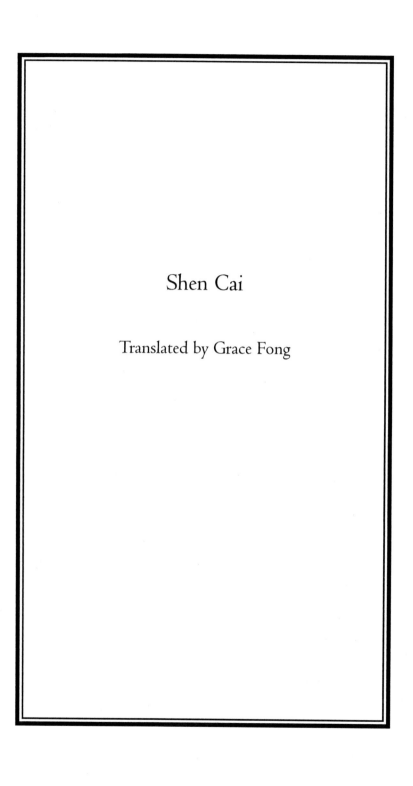

Shen Cai

Translated by Grace Fong

At barely thirteen, Shen Cai (b. 1752) was married as a concubine to scholar and bibliophile Lu Xuan of the wealthy Lu lineage of Pinghu County in Zhejiang province. In his preface to Shen Cai's literary work, *Collection of the Spring Rain Tower*, printed in 1782 when she was thirty, Lu Xuan mentioned that she came from a good family that had fallen on hard times in neighboring Wuxing County. This is all that is known about Shen Cai's background. Concubinage was a practice with a long history in the patriarchal society of imperial China. While a man could only legally marry one principal wife, he could take a number of concubines. The *Record of Rituals* prescribed that when a man reached forty years of age and was still without male offspring, he could take a concubine for procreation to continue the patriline. In social practice, the reasons for taking concubines ranged broadly, but often for sexual indulgence, social status, or even domestic service. Similarly the fates of concubines also varied from the worst suffering at the hands of a jealous principal wife and other concubines to a luxurious and pampered lifestyle provided by doting husbands.

It is not clear in Shen Cai's case why she became a concubine to Lu Xuan at such a young age, but she was a very fortunate concubine. The marriage was not consummated until she was fifteen or sixteen, the female age of maturity set in the *Record of Rituals*. As her poems indicate, Shen Cai in fact grew up under the steady tutelage of Lu Xuan's principal wife, Peng Zhenyin, an accomplished writer of the song lyric, with whom she developed an affectionate relationship. The *Collection of the Spring Rain Tower* is a substantial work of poetry and prose writings. Shen Cai's writings show her to be not only a talented poet in several genres, but also a skillful calligrapher and art connoisseur. She lived a relatively sheltered life in the wealthy Lu household and dedicated her life to the literary arts. Unlike the self-censorship of most gentlewomen who project a persona of virtue and propriety in their writings, the themes and style of Shen Cai's poetry inscribe her perceptions and experience in a language of sensuality and playfulness, a language that is sometimes unabashedly erotic. Her poems on bound feet and smoking tobacco are very unusual subjects in the vast repertory of poetry by women in the Qing dynasty.

GF

Narrated in Jest, Three Poems

I.

Charming and small at thirteen, not knowing names
Learning to make dividing lines, I couldn't quite write
But then I paid respects to a good teacher—the principal wife
Opening the classics, I became a young female scholar

II.

Miles of vernal breeze brighten the Brocade River
A female graduate, top candidate on the examination list
As for judging pupils in the paternal hall of instruction
The Lord of Spring will surely agree to my being a disciple

III.

Dare you hope to go from dullness to high ranks?
When learning characters you must at least remember your names
The rod is imposingly set next to knife and ruler
In giving the children lessons, I am now the female master

Learning Calligraphy

Brush with ivory handle lightly dabbed in a cloud of ink
On a cold day when I tried to copy Yang Xin's style
Before I finished, I lost my grip, the brush tip fell
Soiling my skirt of butterflies in gold appliqué

To the Melody Gazing South of the River: Composed Playfully on Bound Feet (two lyrics)

I.
How ridiculous!
To bend the long jade bows
So tightly bound they grow an underside like a crab
Spread those delicate toes in a row—oh uglier than ginger root
What flavor are they? I ask you, young lover

II.
Girl on the lake—
Her white feet envied by the fish
Crisp and smooth like scallops, shells just cast off
Delicate as lotus shoots, tips first pulled out
After all they are prettier in comparison.

Playful Poem on Springtime Hills

Beyond the tips of apricot trees two jade-white peaks
With a band of thin clouds across and layered green mist
If you want to see the whole body of the delicate hills
Ask Third Master to untie the breast covers

I Laugh at Myself Smoking Tobacco

Could I be a beautiful immortal banished to earth?
But my stomach is not filled with elixirs and ambrosia
Yet I don't desire to eat cooked food
But would sup on a stick of tobacco

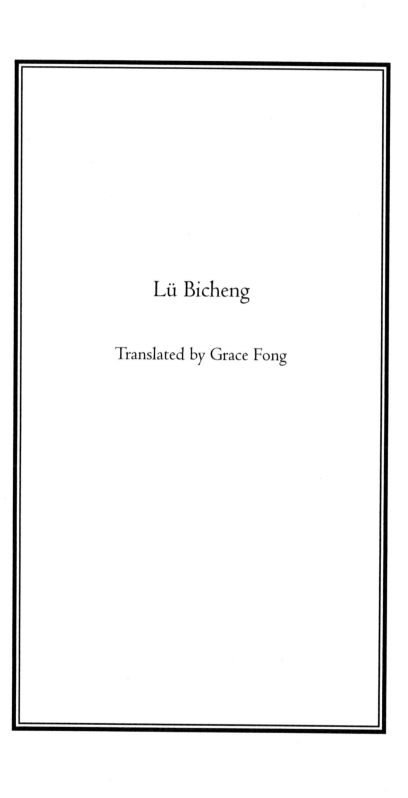

Lü Bicheng

Translated by Grace Fong

The Qing dynasty encountered increasingly serious internal and external threats to its sovereignty in the nineteenth century until it was brought to an end in the 1911 revolution led by Sun Yat-sen, founder of the modern Chinese nation—the Republic of China. In the course of this disastrous century, the Qing state was defeated in the two Opium Wars, the first by Britain (1839-1840) and the second by the joined forces of Britain and France (1856-1860). It was forced to pay heavy indemnities and open up coastal cities such as Shanghai, Guangzhou (Canton), and Tianjin (Tientsin) as treaty ports to the Western powers for trade and commerce, with Hong Kong ceded to Britain in perpetuity in 1842. Internally, the devastating Taiping Rebellion ravaged the country from 1850 to 1865: its armies advanced from south to north, overtaking entire provinces in violent battles with a weakened Qing military and massacring resisting local populations. At the end of the century, the Qing was defeated by the newly rising power of Japan, and north China was devastated by the Boxer Rebellion.

Yet, throughout this period, women's literary culture continued to flourish, undeterred by the widespread violence and social upheaval. Many made poetry into an effective tool for recording, witnessing, and commemorating. Indeed, the broad social, personal, and aesthetic functions of poetry had never been taken to such heights by such a critical mass of women and men of the literati class in the entire history of imperial China.

Born in the waning decades of the Qing to a scholar-official family from Jingde County, Anhui province, the talented Lü Bicheng (1883-1943) and her sisters were taught poetry, calligraphy, and painting as young girls by their parents. Third in birth order, Bicheng became particularly skilled in composing song lyrics. The early death of her father when she was only twelve left the widowed mother and her daughters in a difficult financial situation. The young Bicheng was sent to live with her paternal uncle, an official serving the Qing administration in Tianjin. She came into contact with Western influence and became interested in the new print media of newspapers and periodicals and particularly in new education in schools for women. In 1904, she began to work first as assistant editor for the progressive Chinese newspaper *Dagongbao* (with the French title *L'Impartiel*) and then as principal of the first government-funded girls school, the Beiyang Women's Public School. At the same time, she expressed her personal sentiments in this age of social change, imbuing the literary forms in which she excelled with new ideas and vocabulary. She had her poems and song lyrics published in the *Dagongbao* and the new burgeoning women's journals. She frequently exchanged verses on social occasions with poet friends, government officials, and fellow educators and wrote inscriptions on their paintings and poetry collections. In her twenties at the time, Bicheng had achieved acclaim as a writer of the song lyric. She held that reputation till the end of her ever-changing, half-concealed, half-revealed intriguing life.

Lü Bicheng never married. In the early years of the Republican period, she moved to cosmopolitan Shanghai where she engaged in business with foreigners and amassed a fortune. As an independently wealthy woman, she embarked on international travels in the twenties and thirties, first to America and then to Europe, finally settling down to a reclusive life in the picturesque town of Montreux on the shores of Lake Geneva. She visited the Alps and wrote consummate song lyrics about her experience of European landscape, sending these for publication in journals and newspapers back in China.

In Europe, Bicheng came into contact with the modern Chinese revival of Buddhism led by masters such as Taixu and Yinguang. After she converted, she became a vegetarian and animal protection activist and focused her writings on these subjects. She also began to devote her time to translating Buddhist sutras. She left Europe as the Second World War broke out, intending to return to Shanghai, which, however, had already fallen under Japanese occupation. She spent the last years of her life in Hong Kong, completely devoted to the practice of Buddhism. While she occasionally traveled to Southeast Asia, including Singapore and Penang, Lü Bicheng lived and died at Donglian Jueyuan in Happy Valley,

Hong Kong, a Buddhist temple establishment with a girls' school attached founded by Lady Clara Ho Tung (1875-1938), a friend in religion.

GF

To the Melody A River Full of Red

Stirred by Feelings

Dark has been our country—
I rejoice in the ray of dawn shooting up in the distance.
Who will sing loudly of women's rights?
Joan of Arc.
Eight thousand feet of snow-capped waves, saddened by a sea of
        evil
I look at East Asia in the stormy tide of the twentieth century.
If you hear mad words and weeping coming from my boudoir,
Don't be surprised.

Isolated and confined,
Like the eternity of night.
Fettered and bound,
With no end in sight.
Don't you see me knocking on Heaven's door?
It's hard to unleash my angry feelings.
Far and wide I summon the departed souls to no avail,
I have no way to let splash the hot blood in my chest.
Alas, a frog at the bottom of a well, my wish always denied,
Emotions provoked in vain.

To the Melody Spring in the Drenched Garden

In the seventh month of Dingsi (1917), I visited Mount Lu and stayed at Fairy Glen Lodge, which is translated into Chinese as "Immortal Valley." Perched high in the hollow of the mountain, the scenery is marvelous. The name is quite fitting. After touring around to my heart's content, I am moved to thoughts of leaving this dusty world and composed this lyric on the spur of the moment.

Such an immortal fount—
Only in the human realm
Is the secluded lodge naturally hidden.
Listening to hoary pines in the myriad valleys
They turn into the piping of Heaven even with no wind.
Locked in on all sides by mountain mist,
Though there's no rain it is always dark.
By the winding railing, a flowing rainbow
A high tower rises like a slab of jade—
At times I see the lovely shadow of a startled wild goose.
In the quiet night
The faint sound of the phoenix flute
Flies pass, clear and lofty.

In this floating life how often can I climb up here?
I will gather the misty vines into my arduous verse.
Let the remote footprints roam
For who is host and who guest?
The idle clouds drift—
No past nor present.
Hard it is to summon the yellow crane
For it lingers still among the soft red blooms.
Looking back there is no limit to heaven or the world.
Feeling rueful in vain
How can I prove my past karma?
I want to pay obeisance to the mountain spirit.

To the Melody Recalling the Slave Girl's Charm

Visiting the Ice Mountain Mont Blanc

The Goddess Lingwa at play
Took a twelve-fold crystal screen
And arranged it into precipitous gorges.
Massed angular spikes extending thousands of feet,
An amazing dark and majestic barrier.
Rain smooths the bejeweled branches,
Light bewitches silvery knots,
The luan-bird and crane grieve that they cannot possess it.
The sun goddess Xihe's wheel dares not approach
Its blazing might looks on in vain for eternity.

A picture unrolls over the lake and mountains
Startling my heart at first sight,
But the immortal realm will keep on transforming.
I just fear that Heaven and Earth's energy will be drained
Their color and form shed of all gentle beauty.
Shamanka Gorge barren of clouds
A cold moon over jasper terrace
And dreams end by its spring-like face.
Where are the travelers' footprints?
Could the flying carriage be tied to the end of the sky?

To the Melody Butterflies in the Wind

In mist and haze the three immortal hills are distant,
The vast sea dimmed for thousands of miles.
Although not a winged phoenix,
I am already intimate with Heaven and distant from man.

It's hard to dye the robe with gold powder.
How can I doubt the dream of flowers in the breeze?
How many times can I pace the void?
Except for Ying Hill's glow and its opaque reflection—who
      would know?

Translators' Biographical Notes

MICHAEL FARMAN is a retired electronics engineer. Early in his career he studied Mandarin at the London School of Oriental and African Studies, but began translating Chinese classical and ancient poetry comparatively late in life. Since then, his translations have appeared frequently in literary and translation journals and the anthologies *A Silver Treasury of Chinese Lyrics, 300 Tang Poems,* and *Chinese Erotic Poetry.* His chapbook *Clouds and Rain* was published by Pipers' Ash in 2003. He has organized conference panels and work-shops on Chinese literature and published articles and book reviews in ALTA's *Translation Review.*

GRACE S. FONG is professor of Chinese Literature in the Department of East Asian Studies, McGill University. She received her Ph.D. in classical Chinese poetry from the University of British Columbia. Her research interests encompass classical Chinese poetry and poetics, women writers of late imperial China, and autobiographical writing in pre-modern China. She has con-tributed translations of poems and song lyrics to several antholo-gies of Chinese poetry published in the United States and Hong Kong. She is editor of the Women and Gender in China Studies series published by Brill and Project Director of Ming Qing Women's Writings, an online digital archive and database that began in collaboration with the Harvard-Yenching Library. Her recent publications include the monograph *Herself an Author: Gender, Agency, and Writing in Late Imperial China* (University of Hawaii Press, 2008) and the co-edited volume *The Inner Quarters and Beyond: Women Writers from Ming through Qing* (Brill, 2010).

EMILY GOEDDE received an MFA in literary translation from the University of Iowa. She is currently a Ph.D. candidate in the Department of Comparative Literature at the University of Michigan, where she is researching Chinese poetry from the 1930s and '40s. Her translations have been published in *The Iowa Review,*

227

eXchanges and *Discoveries: New Writing from The Iowa Review*. She also served as co-editor of *eXchanges*, an online journal of literary translation.

JEANNE LARSEN teaches at Hollins University, where she was the inaugural Susan Gager Jackson Professor of Creative Writing; she has studied Tang and pre-Tang poetry in Taiwan, Japan, and the U.S. Her latest book is *Why We Make Gardens, & Other Poems* (Mayapple Press) and her first, *James Cook in Search of Terra Incognita: A Book of Poems* (University Press of Virginia), won the Associated Writing Programs Poetry Series award. Her two books of translations are *Brocade River Poems: Selected Works of the Tang Dynasty Courtesan Xue Tao* (Princeton University Press) and *Willow, Wine, Mirror, Moon: Women's Poems from Tang China* (BOA Editions, Ltd.). The recipient of grants and awards from the NEA, the Japan/U.S. Friendship Commission, the American Council of Learned Societies/Mellon Foundation, and others, she has also published three novels set in an historically imagined China (*Silk Road, Bronze Mirror,* and *Manchu Palaces,* all from Henry Holt); each includes faux translations from Chinese of poems and other texts.

Geoffrey Waters graduated from Vanderbilt University with a B.A. in Chinese and History and received a Ph.D. in Classical Chinese from Indiana University. He became a senior vice president of a California bank. He died suddenly of a heart attack in 2007. His other books of translations include *300 Tang Poems, The Complete Poems of Yu Xuanji, Love Songs of the Sixth Dalai Lama,* and *Three Elegies of Ch'u.*